THE AMERICAN KIN UNIVERSE:
A GENEALOGICAL STUDY

D1611538

David M. Schneider
Calvert B. Cottrell

The University of Chicago Studies in Anthropology
Series in Social, Cultural, and Linguistic Anthropology, No. 3

Published by the Department of Anthropology,
The University of Chicago

1975

Library of Congress Cataloging in Publication Data

Schneider, David Murray, 1918-
  The American kin universe.

  (Series in social, cultural, and linguistic anthropology;
no. 3) (The University of Chicago studies in anthropology)
  Bibliography: p. 101.
  1. Kinship--United States. I. Cottrell, Calvert B., 1940-
joint author. II. Title. III. Series: IV. Series: Chicago.
University. Dept. of Anthropology. The University of Chicago
studies in anthropology.
GN560.U6S35   301.42'1'0973
ISBN 0-916256-02-2
75-37961

The University of Chicago Studies in Anthropology
are available from:
Department of Anthropology
The University of Chicago
1126 East 59th Street
Chicago, Illinois 60637
Price: $5.00 list; $4.00 series subscription

CONTENTS

PREFACE

The material presented here was collected for a study of American
kinship originally conceived as part of a larger, comparative study
of American and British kinship undertaken with Professor Raymond
Firth of the London School of Economics. Further details on the history of the project can be found in Hubert, Forge, and Firth (1967),
Wolf (1964), Firth, Hubert, and Forge (1970), and Schneider (1968).

The major funding for this project came from the National
Science Foundation in two grants. The smaller was specifically provided for the computer analysis of the genealogical material reported
here. In addition, the National Institutes of Health supported certain of the analyses. The support of these agencies is gratefully
acknowledged here.

The fieldworkers who collected the materials analyzed here,
and without whose industrious, intelligent, and conscientious efforts
this work would have not been possible, were Dr. Constance Cronin,
Dr. McGuire Gibson, Dr. Nelson Graburn, Dr. Esther Hermite, Dr. Eliz-
abeth Kennedy, Dr. Charles Keil, Ms. Nan Markel, Mrs. Eleanor McPher-
son, Mrs. Pat Van Cleve, Dr. Harriet Whitehead, and Mrs. Linda Wolf
(now Marks).

We carefully reviewed the literature and considered including
in this monograph systematic comparisons of our findings with those
of other studies on overlapping topics. However, after reviewing
the situation carefully, we realized that, even in the one investigation where some effort had been made to make the work comparable--
the Firth, Hubert, and Forge (1970) study--the results were not analyzed in ways which permitted any meaningful comparisons with ours
to be made.

For example, at the simplest level--the total number of persons included in the kin universe of each informant--this study used
about twice the number of interviews and assembled about twice as
many interview pages of material from about one-half the number of
informants than Firth, Hubert, and Forge (1970). Thus it is hard to
interpret the fact that we report larger kin universes for our American middle-class sample than they do for their London sample, since

v

our informants had twice as much opportunity to report a person. If
the London study had provided the same opportunity to report, perhaps
the figures might have been comparable. But again, where we reported
consanguineals, those married to consanguineals, and the consanguineals of these, for some reason that Firth, Hubert, and Forge do not
explain (see 1970:158), they exclude the last category from the number reported in the kin universe. Hence, even if we compare only
the first two categories, Ego's consanguineals and those married to
them, we know that the American informants had twice as much chance
to report persons as the London informants did. Any comparison thus
becomes problematic. For other studies in the literature, the problems are far greater. Comparisons would be misleading and so we
have chosen to omit them. When and if our methods are replicated,
then the results can certainly be compared. But this is a pilot
study and our aim is less that of trying to establish firm findings
than of pointing to a problem and of outlining certain ways to approach it. Indeed, the work Professor Raymond T. Smith has done
since this study began and with a full knowledge of its details has
already improved on the methods and analysis and has made certain
aims of such a study more precise.

    Finally, a word about how the responsibility for this work is
is distributed between Schneider and Cottrell is in order. Schneider
was the principal investigator. He set the project up and outlined
the kinds of material which the whole American Kinship Project sought.
Cottrell joined the project when the locating interviews were being
conducted. When the genealogical aspects of the intensive work with
the fifty-three families began, Cottrell took immediate charge of
supervising that aspect of the data collection. As each interview
was typed and turned in, Schneider read it and made such comments as
were indicated to the fieldworker. And as the genealogical material
came in, it was Cottrell's responsibility to inspect it and to work
with the fieldworker on it. Inadvertent omissions were often caught
in this way, and the fieldworker could rely on having his material
checked. Often useful leads for directions which the interviews
could take were provided by this supervision of the collection of the
genealogical material. As will be indicated below, it was precisely
this close scrutiny of the data as they were being collected that
led to the discovery of the systematic omission of certain kinds of
materials from the genealogy. This in turn led to the revision of
the methods of supervising, collecting, and recording genealogical
information.

    When the fieldwork was finished, Cottrell set up the code

and supervised the coding crew. They converted the genealogical material into code sheets ready for the puncher, who transferred the material onto IBM cards which were then transferred onto computer tapes. And he was responsible for the basic computer analysis of that material, for designing the runs, and for working directly with the computer technicians to analyze it.

Schneider meanwhile worked with other materials and with the same genealogical material but on other problems.

When Cottrell had finished what he regarded as the basic analytic operations, Schneider joined him in reviewing the analytic work and wrote the first draft of this monograph in the early summer of 1970. Unforeseen events prevented its being completed at that time. It was taken up again in the summer of 1971 but was again halted by events over which none of us had any control. The work was resumed once more in the summer of 1974, when M. H. Schneider took the first two drafts and greatly assisted us in rewriting the entire manuscript. We gratefully acknowledge his help.

INTRODUCTION

I. *Objectives*

The aim of this study is to explore the kin universe of urban, white, middle-class Americans.

The term "kin universe" was first suggested by Firth. It has most recently been defined as "All persons known by our informant (Ego) as related to him by genealogical ties, whether by consanguinity or affinity, i.e., all persons 'recognized' by him as kin" (Firth, Hubert, and Forge 1970:155).

For reasons detailed in chapter 1, we have chosen to modify the definition to include all those claimed as kin as well as those to whom any genealogical tie could be traced by Ego.

II. *Data Collection Procedures*

a. *Creating the "Sample"*

Informants were chosen from the white, urban, middle-class people in Chicago. No other restrictions were placed on the population from which informants could be chosen.

Four different neighborhoods were selected. Experience and census material suggested that these were inhabited predominantly by middle-class whites. Within these neighborhoods, either certain blocks or particular high-rise dwellings were picked at random. The selected areas constitute the pool from which the first random sample of respondents were to be selected for "locating interviews."

The locating interview consisted of a long series of specific questions about age, income, occupation, religious affiliation, number of siblings, number of children, place of birth, length of time resident in present dwelling, ethnic identity claimed, and so on, as well as a number of more open-ended questions on matters relating to kinship and family. In addition, each respondent was asked if he would be interested in further interviews about family and kinship.

The locating interviews provided enough material so that a group of informants could be chosen who were as heterogeneous as possible. A conscious attempt was made to select informants from

every major kind of category and to collect different kinds of data
and different views of the material. Thus, it was important to get
young people without children as well as young people with children,
older people with married children as well as older people without
children, Catholics as well as Protestants, devout Catholics as well
as nominal Catholics, people with small incomes as well as those
with large incomes, those engaged in family businesses as well as
those on salary, etc.

Even if the slightly more than 400 locating interviews we
collected constitutes a sample of some kind, the informants with
whom we finally worked should be described only as a "sample" with
the clear understanding of the limitations and special meaning which
that term has for this study. (See Schneider 1968:12-18 for further
discussion of this.)

The locating interviews took place in the spring and summer
of 1961. The first intensive work with informants began at a very
slow pace during the late fall and winter of 1961. This first period of intensive work (which continued into the spring of 1962)
proved to be an exploratory phase. The material collected proved to
be more useful for discovering and solving problems with the field
methods than for what it contributed as hard data. Some of these
problems will be discussed below. The first period produced a com-
paratively small volume of material, both genealogies and typed interviews.

The succeeding period, from the summer of 1962 through the
fall of 1963 (the last field interview took place in October 1963),
produced the major portion of the data.

b. *Interviewing*

A letter was sent to each prospective family selected from the locating interviews recalling the locating interview and asking if they
would be interested in continuing the study and saying that they would
be telephoned in a few days for their decision. If they were interested in continuing, an appointment with a member of the field team
was set up. The senior author telephoned, gave the name of the fieldworker who would work with the family, arranged the first appointment,
and answered any questions which arose. Assurances of anonymity and
reaffirmation of the scientific goals of the research were given.
The fieldworker would then prepare for his first interview by reviewing the material reported in the locating interview.

The first interview dealt with mutual introductions (only one
member of the team which did the locating interviews continued into

the intensive fieldwork) and any procedural questions the informant raised. Then the fieldworker proceeded.

Except for the opening question of the first interview, the fieldworkers were guided primarily by very broadly stated goals rather than by any set of specific questions to be asked in a given order in prearranged phrasing. Thus the fieldworker had read the guides on weddings, sex role differentiation, genealogy, and so on. His training period and practice interviews had stressed the importance of keeping the very general goal in mind and of avoiding rigid formulations and constructions. The fieldworker had been told to pursue as many different lines as the informant was willing and able to follow and to be patient about certain lines of inquiry, since informants could find them boring or delicate. If this occurred, the fieldworker was to stop pursuing them until opportunity arose later. It was axiomatic that there could be no set number of interviews or set time within which an informant must work. Rather, the number of interviews and the length of time spent with any informant would be determined by his own tolerance for or interest in the topic and our feeling that he had reached the point where he was no longer providing new or useful material.

But the first question *was* fixed and its goals were clearly set. Thus the first interview--except where this proved impossible-- opened with the question: "List for me all those persons whom you consider to be relatives." We called this the "spontaneous listing."[1] The discussion of this list, the inclusions and exclusions, was aimed at developing some notion of the informant's definition of a kinsman or relative. The list also served as the basis for developing the genealogy.

The first interview, then, consisted of Ego's spontaneous listing of relatives, the discussion of why certain persons were or were not included, and then a shift to genealogy. This shift was usually accomplished by indicating that the study was, after all, concerned with family and relatives and that it would be convenient to have a genealogy so that, as different relatives were discussed from time to time, they could be placed. And so the fieldworker suggested that they then proceed to do a genealogy. Usually at this time it was added that, when the genealogy was finished, a neat copy would be made and given to the informant. All informants expressed interest in the genealogy and in having a complete, neat copy, and each was given one when the work was concluded.

The genealogical inquiry proceeded for as long and as steadily as fieldworker and informant found it interesting and tolerable.

Sometimes the informant's interest flagged and a temporary halt was called. This halt could last a few days or even a few weeks, while other subjects were discussed. Some informants, however, remained interested in this inquiry and pursued it almost relentlessly.

In taking the genealogy, the fieldworker elicited certain basic information immediately. As the informant listed a person, the fieldworker learned the individual's name, relationship to the informant, sex, age, religious affiliation, and education. The fieldworker determined whether the person were alive or dead (and, if dead, age at death and year of death), married or not (the name of spouse), occupation, and place of residence. Sooner or later, depending on the fieldworker, the informant, and the situation, certain other information was required about each person on the genealogy. This consisted in data about contact, that is, whether the informant saw that person at weddings, sent Christmas cards, heard from him or telephoned him, and so on.

Fieldworkers were urged to start off with the genealogy just as soon as the spontaneous listing was completed and the inquiry into inclusions and omissions had been pursued as far as it could go without undue pressure. But it must be emphasized that the fieldworker himself was responsible for the conduct of the fieldwork. If, in his judgment, the genealogy was inappropriate, he was to use some other starting point. He was, of course, expected to get a complete genealogy before he finished work with each family.

In fact, each fieldworker did open the first interview with the spontaneous listing, did use this listing as the first step in the collection of genealogical information, and did proceed from the spontaneous listing right into the genealogy. But while some informants were quite prepared to continue until they felt that the genealogy was complete, other informants quickly got bored with genealogical inquiry. Then it became necessary to interrupt the genealogical interviews, turn to other topics and problems, and return to the genealogy from time to time as occasion permitted.

A variety of different attitudes were expressed toward the genealogy itself. Some informants felt a positive pleasure in endlessly listing relatives, remembering their names, ages, occupations, marriages, children, and events in their lives. To others the task seemed dull, routine--a matter of indifference. Some manifested an emphatic ambivalence--one of our informants, a man, said that he didn't know or care, but please be sure to bring him the copy of the genealogy so he could keep it with his important papers.

The genealogy was treated as an open problem for the duration

of our contact with the informant. We did not close it or make a
final copy of it suitable for a parting gift to the informant until
we had completed the last interview. Thus as long as we were with
each informant the names of relatives could be added to his particular genealogy. The point is that the collection of genealogical
material was not confined to one period of the interviewing, nor was
it concentrated into a certain number of sessions. Names could be
added to the genealogy at any time during the course of the work with
the family. Hence there was considerable opportunity for the informant to bring to mind half-forgotten names and dimly remembered persons.

New names for the genealogy came from many different sources.
We collected wedding guest lists, wedding gift lists, funeral atten-
dance books, Christmas card lists, and so on. We then checked these
lists to establish the identity of each name on them. We sometimes
found the names of relatives who had been omitted from the genealogy,
and they were added to it. It was not unusual for the fieldworker
to return for an interview and be greeted by a statement like, "You
remember those cousins I was having so much trouble with last time?
Well, I telephoned Mother and she said . . . " Or the informant
could have consulted a book, a family history, a family bible, or
other relatives. On the other hand, the experience of one fieldworker with one informant was more unusual. The fieldworker arrived
for one of the last interviews with the informant, who was very interested in and proud of the large number of relatives she had. The
fieldworker was met at the door by a housecleaner whom she had never
met before. On being greeted by the informant, the fieldworker at-
tempted a joke: "Well, I suppose that your new housecleaner is a
relative of yours, too!" To which the informant replied, "Yes she
is! And you know, I forgot to mention her!" And so a number of new
relatives, through this one, were added to the genealogy.

We were, of course, interested in the sources other than
those of memory alone that were available to informants for expanding
their kin universe or for obtaining specific information. In some
of our families, certain persons were well-known repositories of just
such information, and these persons prided themselves on their roles
as custodians of family lore. In other families, family histories
had been written and published; and if copies were not immediately
available, their location at least was known. When we began working
with one of our families, historical material about it in a local
library was being actively consulted. A mimeographed family newsletter was being circulated by a member of another informant's fam-

ily--an uncle, in fact. This newsletter contained information about births, death, movements to new locations, and health and illness of family members. It could easily have been consulted by our informant, but this proved unnecessary, since our informant knew just what was in it anyway.

With the exception of published information, all material that informants obtained was recorded on the genealogy and its source identified. When books, published family histories, family newsletters, and massive material of that sort were involved, such sources were identified by title, author, publisher, and date, and these data alone were recorded in the genealogy. Here was part of the answer to the question of where people went who wanted to find out more than they already knew about their kinsmen.

But for our purposes here, the rule for incorporating information was simple. If the material in the genealogy from sources other than the informant's own immediately available knowledge was transmitted to the fieldworker orally, it was coded and used in the analysis. If, however, it was handed to the fieldworker in documents or read directly from published materials, it was not coded and was not included in the analysis. Such materials remain recorded with the primary data and are available for further study, but they are not included here.

All the material contained in the genealogies of our female informants was provided by them orally and directly to the fieldworker. This is not the case for the genealogies of the men. Although we found that husbands, on the whole, were just as willing and eager to be informants as wives, they were nevertheless harder to reach, since they were often busier, had only some evenings free, or were tired after their work day. We tried to talk to and work with the husband in each of our informant families and were mostly successful in doing so. But one device we used to cut down on the amount of time which husbands were asked to spend with the fieldworker was to get as much as possible of his genealogy from his wife. Only then did we ask him to go over it carefully with the fieldworker and go on from that head start. The husband would thus correct, add to, or delete from his wife's basic account. And, indeed, he would bring up relatives to be added to his wife's genealogy as well as to his own. Strictly speaking, then, for our male informants the genealogy represents the combined husband-wife knowledge of the husband's side. Actually, however, we feel confident that our effort to check out each relative with the husband was successful and that we would have had exactly the same information if we had started with him instead of his wife.

c. The Genealogy

From the beginning of the project, fieldworkers were told to gather a total genealogy from each informant--to get (and this is a quotation from the interviewing instructions to each fieldworker) "a complete mapping of the genealogy, defined to include both consanguineal and affinal kin."

There were two reasons for building the interviews around the genealogy. First, the genealogy proved to be sufficiently impersonal to sustain the interview during the development of rapport and trust between the fieldworker and the informant.

Americans consider the genealogy to be quite neutral and matter-of-fact. Blots on the escutcheon can easily be omitted and points of pride stressed. The informant was entirely free in this regard, for the fieldworker was careful not to probe for touchy or delicate material. He simply asked for the names of relatives, how they were related, where they lived, who their husbands, wives, and children were, and so on. This did not prevent the informant from offering small talk and comment. Indeed, informants often availed themselves of the opportunity to chat, so that the fieldworker picked up considerable additional information.

However, in the early interviews, the fieldworker took pains to restrict his questions to such cold facts as names, ages, and places of residence. The fieldworker thus gained the informant's trust and confidence before any tender areas were uncovered. Thus the informant who was suspicious that there were hidden objectives was assured that everything was as simple and straightforward as it seemed. And the informant--and there were a few--who felt convinced that psychological or psychotherapeutic interests were hidden beneath the simple questions was once more assured that such was not the case and that this is what we were really after--Who are your relatives? Where do they live? How often do you see them? What sort of things do you do with them and why? We were *not* interested in offering psychotherapy, or eliciting family secrets, or selling encyclopedias.

Second, the genealogy could be developed as a map of the kin universe, an index of persons to whom attributes could be systematically related. It was a convenient way to order and record the kin universe. As a map, it would immediately show how large the universe was, how far back it went, what and where the boundaries were, who was included or excluded, and so on.

NOTES

1. The "spontaneous listing" was suggested by the late Dr. Millicent Ayoub, who used it in her pioneering studies, at the Fels Research Institute, of the conceptions of family and kinship held by children.

Chapter 1: THE KIN UNIVERSE

I. *Definition and Limits*

According to the rules of American kinship, a potential kin universe
containing an almost infinite number of knowable kin exists for
every person. There is almost no limit to the number of ties of
consanguinity and/or affinity through which the relationship to a
kinsman may be traced. One may count back through the generations
to Adam (or Australopithecus, if one prefers) and include all of
the ancestors of one's own progenitors, their siblings, their siblings' affines, and so on. The set would then include not only direct consanguineals but also persons married to them, and the lat-
ters' consanguineals as well.

From this set a universe of known kin is chosen. This includes kinsmen whom the informant knows or knows of as identifiable
persons. It would not include persons who may be presumed (on the
basis of biological generalizations) to have existed, such as direct
ascendants. Thus the statement, "I must have had four grandparents,
but I have no idea of who they were, I know nothing at all about
them," would exclude the four grandparents. Further, the links may
be consanguineal, persons married to consanguineals (whom we will
henceforth call "affinals"), the consanguineals of those affinals,
and so forth. And the universe would include persons known or be-
lieved to be related, even though the links are unknown or uncertain.
Finally, those to whom genealogical links can be traced but whom
the informant does not consider to be a "relative" may be included.
Thus some informants can trace a link to a brother's wife's sister
and her husband but would not recognize this couple as relatives;
other informants can trace the same links and do recognize them as
relatives. We include all such persons in the kin universe as we
define it. *It is this that we have defined as the kin universe for
the purposes of this study.*

Thus far we have used the terms "potential kin universe" and
"kin universe" or "known kin universe," and before that, the term
"genealogy." In recording material on the genealogy, we took all

9

material which the informant provided *except* that which he provided
or could provide in the form of written or published records. We
must, therefore, to be precise, distinguish between the "kin universe"
and the "genealogy." The sole distinction is the absence of written
or published records in the genealogy. We have nevertheless arbi-
trarily--and possibly unjustifiably--equated the "genealogy" with
the "kin universe" and treated them synonymously throughout this
monograph.

Another subset of the potential kin universe comprises those
persons whom the informant chose to remember and *spontaneously* name
as kinsmen. The specific difference between this subset and what we
have defined as the kin universe is that it is the narrowest definition of relatives that tends to obtain spontaneously among American
informants when probing is kept to a minimum. The word "spontaneously" is the key to this subset, which is the subset which comes
most rapidly to the mind of the unaided informant.

II. *Justification*

Although we worked intensively with fifty-three families, the genealogies of only forty-four were useful for this analysis. It is
worth discussing in some detail exactly why the first nine had to be
excluded. This discussion will also serve to justify our decision
to alter Firth's definition of the kin universe.

A strict interpretation of Firth's definition would people
the kin universe by only a portion of those among the spontaneously
reported few to whom a definite genealogical link could be traced.

In fact, it was exactly such an abbreviated set which was
collected from the first nine families. The kinsmen collected were:
(1) consanguineals with a collateral spread of two to three degrees
and a depth of about three generations or less; (2) spouses of these
consanguineals; and (3) very occasionally, close consanguineals of
these affines.

But while reviewing the material as the fieldworkers brought
it in, we realized that these genealogies were incomplete in the special sense that certain members of the known universe were not being
systematically reported. Individuals such as wife's brother's wife,
uncle's wife's brother, or brother's wife's sister's husband seemed
to be absent.

In addition, fieldworkers returned genealogies on which consanguineal kin were circled, and the informants said that these people were not considered relatives. That is, the informant himself
would trace blood ties to people who he then denied were his rela-

tives. This material came to our attention because the fieldworkers were urged to ask the informant, while inspecting the genealogy, whether there were any persons on it whom he did not consider to be his relatives and why, and then to ask if there were persons they considered to be relatives who were not on the genealogy and why. It was also not unusual for an informant to add persons to the genealogy who were considered to be relatives but whose specific links to him were unknown.

The question, then, is why we got such consistently incomplete and apparently inconsistent results during the first period of fieldwork.

Part of the answer is that at first the fieldworkers did not systematically ask and insist on answers to the routine questions, "And has he any brothers or sisters? mother or father? son or daughter? husband or wife?" If each kinsman listed on the genealogy had been the stimulus for systematically putting such questions, then we are sure that the first nine genealogies would have been more nearly complete.

We therefore instituted a simple system that required the fieldworker to record an X when he had in fact asked those questions and had been told by the informant, "There were none," or "Of course he must have had a mother and father, but I don't know who they were," or "I don't know if he married or not," or "I don't know if he ever had any children or not." That is, the X showed us that the fieldworker said he asked those questions. Once this device had been inaugurated, the fieldworker's failure to so mark a terminal kinsman would cue the supervisor to remind him to follow up that line at his next opportunity. Before the fieldworker's last interview with any family, the genealogical material was reviewed to determine whether the Xs were all there and no loose genealogical ends remained. This routine was certainly not foolproof, but we feel that its systematic use assured us of a far higher level of validity than we had had before we instituted it.

In order to understand our decision to collect the largest possible set of kin, the reader must allow two points. The first is that both the "known" and the "spontaneously selected" sets are legitimate, meaningful units in the cultural rules of American kinship. The second is that, for this preliminary survey, the larger set would provide the greatest amount of generally useful information.

The set of people that the fieldworker collects on the genealogy is the concrete outcome of a series of choices which have been made about whom to include as a relative and whom to exclude. Some

of these choices are made by the informant and some by his forebears,
but all are made according to the rules of American kinship. If
these rules permitted no choice whatever, we would be able to pre-
dict precisely who would be included on the genealogy and who would
be excluded--except where the informant broke the rules or failed to
remember everyone. But the rules of American kinship in this matter
are such that different choices are equally proper and legitimate.
Hence it is only by knowing the probability that one kind of choice
will be made over another, or by knowing what conditions tend to favor certain choices over others, that we can make accurate predic-
tions about the content of a given genealogy. (This statement as-
sumes that eliciting procedures are appropriate and have no effect.)

The rules of American kinship define the cultural category
of "a relative" as a person related "by blood" or "by marriage," but
both of these terms have at least two meanings. (For a full discussion of these definitions, see Schneider 1968.) "Blood" means shared
biogenetic substance. But it also means "a relationship" in the
sense of an interpersonal relationship which is governed by a particular code for conduct, a code that enjoins diffuse, enduring solidarity. But in addition, "marriage" can be more narrowly marked to
mean the relationship of marriage between any consanguineal and a
person of the opposite sex, and even more narrowly marked to mean
only the marriage of Ego, the informant--thereby excluding persons
married to consanguineal relatives. These meanings are modified by
a rule of "distance," so that two kinds of relatives emerge. One is
a set of "close" relatives, the other a set of "distant" relatives.
"Close" blood relatives share more biogenetic substance than "distant" blood relatives. Thus mother, father, brother, sister, son,
and daughter are "close blood relatives," while a cousin's cousin is
not. Yet a cousin's cousin is, of course, closer than a cousin's
cousin's cousin. The point is that there is no clear-cut, absolute
boundary within which all are equally "relatives" and outside which
all are equally not. By the same token, the degree to which choice
is possible is smaller the closer the relative is, and greater the
more distant the relative is. The distance rule functions as a device for closure or exclusion, but just where it will be applied is
not given either in the rule or in the definition of the category of
"relatives."

Given this fourfold definition, anyone can properly and le-
gitimately use one or another or some combination of these elements
to justify his decision to include or to exclude a particular person
from the category, "my relative." Thus he may volunteer the name of

a particular person for the genealogy, showing the particular consanguineal connection, yet say that "He is not a relative of mine" because he is "too far away, and I never see him anyway." (Meaning, of course, that they do not have a personal relationship.) Similarly, Ego may develop a further set of alternate choices out of the marked meaning of "marriage." "By marriage" can be used to mean that two persons are married to each other, and if I am related to one as a blood relative, I am related to the other, who is married to him, "by marriage." Thus I may be related to my brother's wife "by marriage." But am I related to my brother's wife's mother "by marriage"? Some informants say "Yes, because she is your brother's mother-in-law, and you are related to your brother, aren't you?" But others can with equal cogency say, "She is your brother's mother-in-law, not yours!" And of course the next step is brother's wife's mother's sister. Is she related to me "by marriage" or is she only my sister-in-law's aunt--certainly not mine? Finally, the question may be resolved in yet another way. Ego may affirm quite emphatically that he *is* related to the lady in question as she is, after all, his brother's wife's aunt, and they have very warm, positive feelings about her. "After all, she was so good to my sister-in-law when she was a child . . . " And so they do indeed--all of them--count the dear, sweet soul as one of their closest relatives.

It is certainly true that some of these choices are not often made. One consideration which bears on the frequency with which certain choices are made is that "blood" is closer than "marriage," and the claims of those who are "closer" are stronger than the claims of those who are "distant." Thus the spouse of a consanguineal is "closer," *other things being equal*, than the consanguineal of the spouse of a consanguineal. This is reflected in the fact that our spontaneous listings contain mostly consanguineals (hereafter designated as C). Next in frequency come spouses of consanguineals (hereafter designated as CA, "consanguineal's affinal"). Consanguineal's affinal's consanguineal (CAC) appears more rarely. Unless they have some good reason to, informants generally do not tend to think of CAC as "relatives" or as being "related to me." Yet, as we have been trying to make clear, such a person may or may not be counted as a relative, according to the definitions of this category in American culture. And either of these alternate courses is an equally legitimate and proper way of following the rules of American kinship.

But it is most important that we do not confuse the question of whether such choices are legitimate and proper according to the rules of American kinship with the question of how rarely they may occur. Because a particular choice is not often made does not mean that it is wrong or improper; it means only that it is not often made.

It was just this confusion which dominated our thinking during the early stages of the fieldwork--and dominated the thinking of our fieldworkers and informants as well. It also biased the formulation and operation of our eliciting procedures. Wherever fieldworkers were instructed to be exhaustive, they were also instructed to get all the "consanguineal and affinal" kin. The way such instructions are followed depends on the fieldworker's understanding of those terms. And so the fieldworker would get a relative like a mother's brother onto the genealogy, think of him as a consanguineal or "blood relative," find out about his wife, think of her as an affine or "relative by marriage," go on to their children, and figure that the job was done. Because CAC are not consistently counted as relatives, fieldworkers and informants alike did not take active steps to see, first, if they even existed.

Thus, we have chosen to discover and study the entire group of people who met only two criteria: (a) they were known to the informant; and (b) they could, according to the cultural definitions, be considered relatives *if the informant so chose.* Since we collected numbers of people whom the informants specifically disavowed as relatives, this monograph cannot be taken strictly as a study of that cultural category as each of our informants actually used it. Each genealogy we collected was usually larger, in greater or lesser degree, than the particular informant's definition of his universe of relatives. We must distinguish, therefore, between any given informant's *kin universe* and his *universe of relatives.* The latter is selected from the former; the former is the largest universe from which the latter can be drawn. This work is a study of the kin universe and not a study of the subset of that universe--the universe of those actually counted as relatives by each informant.

Why did we choose to study the kin universe rather than the universe of relatives? First, we wanted to know about the largest available universe from which our informants could, at any time, select their relatives. Second, we discovered that we would have missed a large and significant segment of relevant data if we had proceeded in any other way.

Let us make the first point in yet another way. The kin universe as we have defined it is precisely the same as the definition of the American cultural category of "relatives," *except that it omits any device of closure or exclusion.* The device of closure or exclusion is the American cultural concept of "distance." (This is more fully discussed in Schneider 1965, 1968.) Our aim in the study was to discover what kinds of persons are included in the universe from which the actual universe of relatives is chosen at any time. Not "why," but "who"; what kinds are in and what kinds are out.

By altering our eliciting procedures and by working more rigorously and systematically, we did in fact obtain larger kin universes from our informants than we would have if we had continued as we began. If we consider one particular case in some detail, we can see this.

To begin with, consider the last row of table 1.1. Of the total genealogy, 116 out of 387, or 30%, are consanguineal kin. Fifty-eight, or 15%, are CA (consanguineals' affinal, i.e., persons married to any of Ego's consanguineals), but 213, or 55%, of the total genealogy are CAC+ (consanguineals' affinals' consanguineals and beyond, or plus, that is, the consanguineals of persons married to Ego's consanguineals and those more distantly related).

Since we shall be using the symbols C, CA, CAC, and CAC+ throughout this work, it would be well to be specific in defining them. C, as we have indicated, means "consanguineals," and thus mother, father, brother, sister, son, daughter, grandmother, grandfather, etc. would count as C. A stands for affinal and it is used only after C; thus the full term is CA and means anyone married to anyone counted by Ego as a consanguineal. It would include a mother's brother's wife, a brother's wife, a sister's husband. It would also, of course, include Ego's own spouse, and so the spouse's brother would be a CAC. CAC means anyone who is a consanguineal's spouse's consanguineal, or consanguineal's affinal's consanguineal. The designation + simply means "and all beyond that point." Thus CA chains can go on indefinitely; C, CA, CAC, CACA, CACAC, etc. CAC+ includes the CAC plus all related through such a person, regardless of how far the chain extends.

The other rows provide a partial breakdown of these figures. First, contrast rows 3 and 6. Row 3 contains all kin listed through parents. Hence CAC in this row are linked to Ego through an initial consanguineal chain of at least two kin types. Row 6 contains all linked through siblings and children; thus all CAC are linked through an initial consanguineal chain of one or more kin types.

To analyze these data in another way, we recognize that it is through relatives in the CA column that relatives in the CAC+ column are incorporated into the kin universe. In row 6, 17 consanguineals' spouses bring in 188 CAC+ kinsmen, or about 11 CAC+ for

16

Table 1.1

Case 05

	C	CA	CAC+	Total
1. Through mother . . .	31	19	0	50*
2. Through father . . .	32	22	25	79
3. Through parents . .	63	41	25	129
	49%	32%	19%	100%
4. Through children . .	9	2	19	30
5. Through siblings . .	44	15	169	228
6. Through siblings and children	53	17	188	258
	20%	7%	73%	100%
Total	116	58	213	387
	30%	15%	55%	100%

* Ego's mother's siblings all died before reaching maturity. Hence, all but four of the total of fifty are Ego's mother's parents' siblings, their spouses and children, these children's spouses and children, etc.

each consanguineal's spouse; whereas in the more distant collateral lines shown in row 3, 41 consanguineals' spouses bring in only 25 CAC+, that is, fewer than one CAC+ per consanguineal's spouse.

Finally, rows 1 and 2 provide two contrasts: (1) between the sex of the primary linking relative; and (2) between the descent lines of parent's siblings and parent's parent's siblings (observe the note).

Though it could be shown that more persons can be included in the genealogy, the question remains of whether this would do anything more than increase the size of the kin universe. Are the CAC+ really important in any way beyond the fact that they may be known to exist? One measure of this is the types of contact shown in table 1.2.

Table 1.2

Case 05

	1st Cousins	CAC+ through Children	CAC+ through Husband's Siblings	CAC+ through Ego's Siblings	Total CAC+ through Siblings	Total CAC+
1. Number of visits to members of this category	0	0	6	4	10	10
2. Number of seeing contacts to members of this category . .	0	12	28	71	99	111
3. Number of phone calls to members of this category	0	6	6	37	43	49
4. Number of letters to members of this category	0	0	0	2	2	2
5. Number of Christmas cards to members of this category	1	5	1	2	3	8
6. Number in this category seen at formal occasions	7	0	1	11	12	12

Rows on the chart designate types of interaction. The distinction between rows 1 and 2 is that visits are face-to-face contacts between Ego and a kinsman which are *desired, planned, and initiated* by Ego or that kinsman; for example, going to each other's house or going out to dinner together. However, "seeing" contacts are those instances of face-to-face contact that are the result of chance or of the action of others. In the last row, "formal occasions" refers to such ceremonies as wakes, weddings, funerals, confirmations, bar mitzvahs, etc. All other rows are self-explanatory.

Columns present certain categories of Ego's kin universe—first cousins and various types of CAC kin. Numbers in the cells are the frequencies of interaction per year.

Now, the large proportion of Ego's interaction with her kin universe is with her children and their families, her siblings and their families, and her deceased husband's siblings and their families. These constitute the nucleus of her kin contacts.

Table 1.2 is concerned with the periphery of Ego's interaction sphere. It focuses on the question of which categories, compared with first cousins, supply contacted kin. Kinsmen on this chart are all tertiary or more distant (note that CAC must be at least tertiary kin). Ego has eight first cousins living in the Chicago area. While she knows of the existence of more distant cognates, she has contact with none of these; hence, column 1 is limited to consanguineal kin of the same generation and two degrees of collateral removal.

There is no need to go through table 1.2 in detail. Let us simply note that, *in all rows, contact with CAC kin is greater than contact with cousins.* Cousins are seen only at formal occasions, and only one Christmas card is sent to a person in this category. In contrast, CAC kin are visited, seen, and telephoned a substantial number of times a year.

By the time we had finished the genealogies of the first nine families, we realized that the CAC+ category could well be very important. Using the last two tables, we offer one more reason.

When we began the study, we felt intuitively that it was obvious that, if sib-set size were held constant, there was only one way any Ego could expand the size of his kin universe. This was to go back a greater number of generations and to incorporate more distant collateral lines. Now, our informant in case 05 (tables 1.1 and 1.2) has knowledge of only one of four grandparental sib-sets. Members of this sib-set and relatives linked through them add only 44 to a kin universe of 387 persons, or about 12% of the total. The

first table, then, indicates in extreme form the importance of one
alternative that we did not anticipate. That is that Ego can go
through consanguineals' spouses, especially the spouses of close
consanguineal kin, and bring into the kin universe the consanguineals
of these, thus increasing the kin universe's size considerably. In
other words, in carving an effective kin unit out of her total kin
universe, our informant does not follow cognatic lines beyond the
primary and secondary kin. Rather, she goes through the spouses of
consanguineals and incorporates their consanguineals as well.

Thus, by insisting on collecting the entire universe of
known kin, we have discovered a large set of people who are important both to our informants and to our understanding of American kinship.

Chapter 2:   GUIDE TO THE DATA AND ANALYSIS

I. Description of the Sample

As we have indicated, we worked intensively with fifty-three families,
but the first nine did not provide genealogies full enough to be used
here. The usable genealogies came from forty-four families. Of the
informants for these, one was a widow and one a divorcee. In two
cases, we were not satisfied with the material from the husbands.
Hence, the eighty-four genealogies presented here were obtained from
forty husband-wife pairs and four additional women.

It was neither desirable nor possible to make all computations from the same pool of informants. For certain calculations
(for example, when we tested to see if women knew more kin on mother's
side than on father's side), all forty-four women were considered.
However, for certain other calculations (for instance, when the pur-
pose of the analysis was to compare husbands with wives), only the
forty matched pairs were counted.

Moreover, of these forty husband-wife pairs, only thirty-
nine provide adequate information about frequency of contact with
kin. Finally, despite all our efforts, there is reasonably complete
information on the CAC+ category for only twenty-nine. Our various
subsamples and their uses are:

	Subsample	*Purpose*
1)	84 individual Egos: 40 men and 44 women	For discussion of data in the C and CA categories where husband-wife comparison is not essential.
2)	80 individual Egos: 40 husbands and 40 wives	For discussion of data in the C and CA categories where husband-wife comparison is made.
3)	58 individual Egos: 29 husbands and 29 wives	For discussion of the place of CAC+ in the kin universe.
4)	78 individual Egos: 39 husbands and 39 wives	For discussion of contact frequen-cies.

Our fifty-three families gave us over 500 interviews, which
ran to more than 6,300 pages of typescript. However, we had more

21

than twice as many interviews with wives as with husbands, including
the four unpaired women. The amount of interview material was similarly distributed. About twice as many pages recorded the wife's
interview as were taken up with information from the husband. By
these measures, then, we have twice as much information for women as
for men. We saw and talked with women twice as often as men, and
women had twice the chance that men did to provide us with material.

Under these circumstances, it may seem preposterous for us
to use our unadjusted figures to compare men and women. However,
we recognized this difficulty in the course of the interviewing, and
through the use of the techniques described above, we believe that
we have produced comparable data sets. The compensation was probably
imperfect. But given the exploratory nature of this study, that im-
perfection is probably totally obscured by other, grosser imperfections.[1]

The fifty-three families we worked with were selected from
four different parts of Chicago.[2] We have already said that we chose
areas of Chicago that were predominantly white middle class. Area 1
was an old development of single-family dwellings characterized by
older families with grown and half-grown children and incomes ranging
up from $10,000 a year. This area provided fifteen informant fami-
lies. Area 2 was a new development of single-family dwellings where
houses sold for about $10,000-$15,000. It was inhabited primarily
by young couples, with small children, whose incomes tended to go to,
but not often above, about $15,000 a year. Eighteen informant fami-
lies came from this area. Area 3 consisted of a series of high-rise
apartment buildings on the Chicago lakefront. Here we encountered a
mixture of older and younger families. They had higher incomes than
the inhabitants of area 2 but were apartment rather than house dwell-
ers. Area 4, which provided two families, was a high-density, high-
rental street of high-rise apartments at the edge of the downtown
area. Here incomes well over $30,000 a year were usual, although we
found a few that were lower. In this area we also found a mixture
of both younger and older families. The remaining three informant
families came from other suburban, single-family dwelling areas of
Chicago.

The last three informant families lead us to the next point
about our informants--some of them were related to each other as parent and child or as siblings. More specifically, one of the informant families from area 4 contained the father and mother of two of
the families elsewhere in Chicago through the husbands in each. That
is, the family from area 2 had two married sons, and we worked in-

tensively with each married son (and his family) as well as with the
parental family. The third family from elsewhere provided the reverse situation. The wife in one of our informant families from area
2 suggested that we try her mother and father. We did, and so worked
intensively with them as well as with their daughter and her husband.
Two of the families in area 3 were related as mother and father and
married daughter and her husband. In sum, the genealogies of these
forty-four families are unrelated to each other except in seven families where there are parents and two married sons (three families)
and parents and married daughter (four families, each pair unrelated
to the other pair). In each case, we have treated the genealogy of
each husband and of each wife both as a married pair and as an independent male or female informant; and we have ignored the relationship between the families.[3]

Most of the families had either two or three children; the
range was from none to nine.

Table 2.1

Number of Children per Family

Number of Children	Number of Families	Number of Children	Number of Families
0	4	5	1
1	4	6	2
2	15	7	1
3	14	8	1
4	1	9	1

Of our forty-four families, eleven were Catholic, nine Jewish, four Congregational, five Episcopal, four Presbyterian, three
Lutheran, three Methodist, one Unitarian, one Mennonite, one Mormon,
one Greek Orthodox; one family said it had no religious affiliation.

By income, our families were distributed as shown in table
2.2.

The attitudes about their ethnicity of our forty-four families may be characterized as follows. Certain families took a positive view of their ethnic identities. Six families were concerned
with their Jewish identity and actively maintained it. One family

24

Table 2.2

Annual Family Income

Annual Income (U.S.$)	Number of Families	Annual Income (U.S.$)	Number of Families
under 5,000	0	15-19,999	7
5-7,999	3	20-24,999	4
8-9,999	9	25-29,999	2
10-14,999	12	30 and over	7

was equally concerned with its identity as Italian-American, one as Greek-American, three as Irish-American, one as Czech-American, one as German-American. The remainder viewed ethnicity without positive concern. This remainder comprised those whose parents had been born in America or in Canada, Hungary, Sweden, Holland, Denmark, Wales, England, Germany, Yugoslavia, Turkey, and Scotland.

II. *Description of the Analysis*

A number of fundamental decisions were made early in the analysis. The reader should know of them before attempting to understand the data.

Every husband has a genealogy that is distinct from that of his wife if they were not related to each other before their marriage. And after marriage, of course, each husband can trace a connection through his wife to all of those people who are on her genealogy. The wife can similarly trace a connection through her husband.

We have arbitrarily separated the two genealogies at Ego's marriage bond. Thus, we have not counted a man's wife's consanguineals and their affines as *his* CA or CAC+ or vice versa.

In addition, where a husband-wife pair each contributes a genealogy, a set of relatives are held in common. These include children, grandchildren, their spouses, and the CAC+ through them. For younger married couples without children, this set may have no members. But for older informants with several married children, the the number of members in this set can easily reach the hundreds.

For certain husband-wife comparisons, we simply ignored this set. On the other hand, for calculations such as absolute size, we included this set with *both* husband and wife. This is indicated on the appropriate tables.

There is a definite hazard here for the unwary reader. Figures must not be added indiscriminately, or this set may well be
accorded outstanding significance by being counted twice.

In order to avoid this, we coded and punched all children
and people related through children only on the wife's genealogy.
Hence they *never* appear in summaries of Ego male except where specifically indicated, and they are always included in Ego female except where explicitly excluded.

Finally, step-, adopted, and half- relatives, as well as
those to whom no link can be traced, are all *excluded* from our calculations. This is discussed below, under "Step-, Half-, Adopted,
and Link Unknown."

Generally, an adequate statement of the American genealogy
describes the kinds of persons that make up the kin universes of our
informants and the proportions in which they occur. We have approached these problems in two ways. In the first, our unit of analysis is the individual case. Here we will consider questions like,
How large is the kin universe? What proportion of the kin universe
are consanguineals, spouses of consanguineals, kin more distant in
affinal linkage? Do our female informants have larger genealogies
than our males? Does the age of the informant correlate with family
size, proportion of living kin on the genealogy, amount of contact
with extranuclear family kin? For each such problem in our analysis,
the basic datum will be the individual informant and his genealogy--
its size, the proportion who are living, named, visited, telephoned,
consanguineal, etc.

In our second approach, we summarize our informants' genealogies (or specified subsets of these) and analyze the ways in which
these sums are distributed throughout the cells generated by the in-
tersection of the dimensions of generation and collateral removal.
Here the basic datum is the cell frequency. How many kin in a given
cell (first cousins, for example) are known to exist? What proportion of these are named, contacted, married, etc.? How do these
values compare with values in the same items in other cells (parents'
first cousins, own first cousins' children, etc.)?

Throughout the ensuing analysis, our informants will be strat-
ified according to two major variables--sex and age. Comparing the
compositions of male informant's and female informant's kin universes
is an understandable tactic. Our informants were in almost complete
agreement that women knew more about kinship and were more involved
with kin than men. We shall demonstrate below that sometimes this
is true and sometimes it is not.

Stratifying our informant population by age is a conventional sociological maneuver. Age has considerable effect on some of our variables.

The ages of our informants are listed in tables 2.3 and 2.4, according to their membership in the three age categories we have used.

Table 2.3

Sample Characteristics

Sample for C and CA Purposes	Young	Middle	Old
Sample size	14	13	13
Mean age husband	32.9	43.2	56.5
Age range husband	28-37	38-49	50-70
Mean age wife	29.2	38.8	53.4
Age range wife	26-31	32-45	49-58

Sample for Contact Purposes	Young	Middle	Old
Sample size	14	13	12
Mean age husband	32.9	43.2	56.5
Age range husband	28-37	38-49	50-70
Mean age wife	29.2	38.8	53.4
Age range wife	26-31	32-45	49-58

Sample for CAC+ Purposes	Young	Middle	Old
Sample size	10	11	8
Mean age husband	32.5	42.5	57.4
Age range husband	28-37	38-49	50-70
Mean age wife	29.5	39.5	54.3
Age range wife	28-31	33-45	50-58

Table 2.4

Informants' Ages

	Young			Middle			Old	
Case #	Husband	Wife	Case #	Husband	Wife	Case #	Husband	Wife
01*	33	30	02	49	41	03	70	58
04	30	29	06	42	38	05*	. .	58
08	28	28	07	37	35	09	51	52
10*	31	26	11	47	43	14	51	51
12	38	28	16	43	45	17	59	56
13	32	29	18	39	36	19*	49	51
15	34	30	20	42	41	21	60	57
25*	35	27	22	49	41	24*	52	49
28*	36	31	23	49	41	27*	60	55
30	32	31	26*	45	32	29*	58	52
33	31	30	31	39	33	37	54	54
34	31	30	32	41	41	39	53	50
35*	. .	27	38*	. .	43	42*	56	56
36	37	31	40*	39	38	43	61	56
41*	31	28						
44	32	29						

* Informants excluded from set of 29 matched husband-wife pairs.

Table 2.5

Categories Normally Excluded from Computations

Family Number	Husband			Wife				
	Half-, Step*	All Other†	Total	Half-, Step	Child	Grandchild, Uncoded¶	All Other	Total
01	2	71	73	1	2	0	130	133
02	5	136	141	8	4	4	177	193
03	6	185	191	0	3	39	101	143
04	16	61	77	10	3	0	85	98
05	5	5	5	20	3	40	346	409
06	5	199	204	13	9	2	322	346
07	6	82	88	5	3	2	137	147
08	8	55	63	12	2	2	151	167
09	25	209	234	113	8	8	468	597
10	9	215	224	1	2	2	236	241
11	21	313	334	35	3	30	239	307
12	3	106	109	16	2	1	100	119
13	17	28	45	39	2	0	90	131
14	10	244	254	6	2	17	192	217
15	1	136	137	1	6	6	123	136
16	4	97	101	7	0	1	96	104
17	18	138	156	0	2	17	174	193
18	8	191	199	17	3	1	100	121
19	1	65	66	6	2	2	103	113
20	0	23	23	21	2	6	35	64
21	40	134	174	29	2	39	246	316
22	2	23	25	21	3	9	167	200
23	30	128	158	8	6	3	178	195

24	30	138	168	21	2	3	109	135
25	0	90	90	14	2	0	165	181
26	7	104	111	14	1	6	208	229
27	18	77	95	3	3	8	124	138
28	5	130	135	1	7	13	78	99
29	21	146	167	32	3	2	144	181
30	11	36	47	5	1	6	193	205
31	35	130	165	16	1	7	245	269
32	99	314	413	2	5	4	230	241
33	17	74	91	30	3	5	155	193
34	3	128	131	6	0	1	56	63
35	§	§	§	25	0	2	76	103
36	13	59	72	3	2	4	186	195
37	26	152	178	25	3	18	74	120
38	§	§	§	0	2	11	121	134
39	3	101	104	22	3	35	421	481
40	2	62	64	29	2	0	109	140
41	§	§	§	54	1	1	76	132
42	2	100	102	0	0	1	146	147
43	137	269	406	161	2	137	395	695
44	7	166	173	29	3	3	94	129
Total	673	5,115	5,788	881	120	498	7,401	8,900
Mean	16.8	128	144.5	20.0	2.7	11.3	168	202
N	40	40	40	44	44	44	44	44

* Half-, step-, adopted, link unknown.

† Totals on which computations are usually based.

¶ Grandchild, CA+ through these, and those CA chains from the genealogy that proved to be uncodable. Hence, even when the "child" column says 0, figures here may be present as uncodable CA chains.

§ No genealogy.

III. Step-, Half-, Adopted, and Link Unknown

In the preliminary stages of this analysis, we decided to exclude
from consideration all those people on the genealogy who were not
simple C, CA, or CAC+. Those excluded were step-relations, adopted
kin, and half-kin, as well as all persons the informant claimed as
kin but to whom the informant could trace no link.

We did so for two reasons. First, those excluded constitute
a peculiar, widely variable catchall category. Its numbers could
fluctuate because of accidents of death, remarriage, sterility, or
other idiosyncratic causes. We felt that by simply excluding the
whole category we would do much to compensate for such accidents.
Moreover, the computational difficulties that would have been intro-
duced by including this one small category seemed to outweigh its
significance by far.

In retrospect, it is easy to criticize this decision. As we
have pointed out, it is important to consider the complete genealogy
as an integrated whole. We could as easily have excluded all persons
related through father's siblings on the ground that in certain cases
the father was an only child--yet this would hardly seem reasonable.
However, we shall offer our results despite this admitted imperfec-
tion.

To enable the reader to gauge the consequences, the actual
number of excluded individuals and brief summary statistics are presented in table 2.5.

One obvious consequence of excluding this assemblage of persons is that we have reduced the size of the total sample by between
10% and 11%. Further, we do not know what effect this exclusion has
had on any of our findings, for we do not know what biases this group
might have shown. We did not, and cannot now, examine it to see.
Whether including this assemblage would have altered any of our findings significantly is simply unknown, and this is a serious qualifi-
cation on all of our results.

NOTES

1. See pp. 23-30 for other imperfections.

2. While we were selecting the fifty-three families with whom
we wanted to work intensively, we had eleven refusals.

3. A special study was undertaken of what we have called "peel-
ing," that is, the question of what part of a parent's genealogy is
given by a child. Thus we went out of our way to find parent and
child and siblings whose genealogies we could compare in this way.
This study will be reported elsewhere.

Chapter 3: THE RESULTS

I. *Size*

The number of people in our informants' kin universes is widely variable and associated with both the age and the sex of the informant.

Our sample consists of twenty-nine husband-wife pairs for whom we have adequate information in the CAC+ category.

The figures in this section do *not* include Ego's children. Nor are people related through children, e.g., grandchildren; and sons- or daughters-in-law and their consanguineals are not counted. They are excluded because their number is largely a function of whether the informant's children are married. A married child brings in not only his own spouse but the spouse's consanguineals (CAC) and the affines of those (CACA), and so on. Thus a family with two young, unmarried children will have only two people excluded, whereas a family with two married children might exclude a considerable number.

In fact, by this exclusion our smallest kin universe (23) has excluded eight persons, our largest (468) has excluded sixteen, while our third largest (395) has excluded one hundred and nine.

Table 3.1 presents a brief statistical summary of the data. Table 3.2 shows the distribution of sizes by age and sex.

From inspection of these tables, one would expect wives to tend to have larger kin universes than their husbands. This is confirmed by a Wilcoxen matched pairs signed rank test comparison of husbands with wives, $p<.05$. However, it must be remembered that, although the wife's kin universe was larger than the husband's in eighteen cases, the opposite was true in the other eleven.

It would also appear that older persons have larger kin universes than younger persons. This observation is supported by table 3.3, which yields a $Chi^2 = 9.18$, with $.01<p<.02$.

In sum, the kin universes of our informants range from 23 persons, the smallest, to 504, the largest (including children, grandchildren, etc.). Most, however, run between 51 and 200 persons, and wives generally, but by no means always, have larger kin universes than their husbands. Older people report more relatives than younger

31

32

Table 3.1

Summary of Kin Universe Sizes
by Age and Sex of Informant

	Young	Middle	Old	Total
Male				
Mean	85	147	179	135
Median . . .	67	130	168	130
Range . . .	28–166	23–314	101–269	23–314
Number . . .	10	11	8	29
Female				
Mean	117	175	259	183
Median . . .	111	177	219	183
Range . . .	56–193	35–322	74–468	35–468
Number . . .	10	11	8	29
Total				
Mean	110	161	219	159
Median . . .	97	152	188	136.5
Range . . .	28–193	23–322	74–468	23–468
Number . . .	20	22	16	58

Table 3.2

Distribution of Kin Universe Sizes
by Age and Sex of Informant

Kin Universe Size	*Young* M	F	*Middle* M	F	*Old* M	F	*Total* M	F
0–50 . .	2		2	1			4	1
51–100 . .	4	5	2	2		1	6	8
101–50 . .	3	1	3	1	3	1	9	3
151–200 . .	1	4	2	3	2	2	5	9
201–50 . .				3	2	1	2	4
251–300 . .					1		1	
301–50 . .			2	1			2	1
351+ . . .						3		3
Total . .	10	10	11	11	8	8	29	29

Table 3.3

Size of Universe by Age of Informant

Universe Size	Young (N=20)	Middle (N=22)	Old (N=16)
Number of cases below median* . . .	15	10	4
Number of cases above median . . .	5	12	12

* Median=136.5.

people, and older women usually have the largest kin universes (with important exceptions, of course). Three general questions are raised by these results. First, what factors contribute to increased kin universe size? Second, what factors contribute to the fact that women report more kin than men? Third, is the increase in kin universe size with age limited to certain types of kin? The following sections will provide some answers.

II. *Consanguineals and Affinals*

We have noted that the kin universes of our informants can be partitioned into three categories: consanguineals (C); their affinals (CA); and the consanguineals and additional relatives of those affines (CAC+) (see p. 15). In this section, we examine how that partitioning changes with respect to the sex and age of our informants as well as to the total size of the universe.

We have chosen to measure this partitioning by simply dividing the number of persons in each category by the total number on the genealogy. We thus obtain three figures--%C, %CA, and %CAC+. The difficulty of this approach is that, while it appears to provide three distinct, independent, comparable variables, it does not do so. For if one knows the value of any two percentages the third is determined.

Table 3.4 presents our data. These data are summarized in table 3.5. Table 3.6 is intended to convey an impression of the distribution of percentages. These tables suffer from the difficulty noted above, and it should be remembered that the chart should sum to 5,800% at the lower right.

Table 3.4

Number and Percentage of C, CA, and CAC+
by Category, Sex, and Age

Case	*Males* C		CA		CAC+		*Females* C		CA		CAC+	
	N	%	N	%	N	%	N	%	N	%	N	%
02	44	32	17	13	75	55	95	54	48	27	34	19
03	107	58	59	32	19	10	64	63	37	37	0	0
04	35	57	18	30	8	13	46	54	19	22	20	24
06	107	54	32	16	60	30	106	33	28	9	188	58
07	35	43	18	22	29	35	40	29	18	13	79	58
08	32	58	15	27	8	15	46	31	18	12	87	56
09	95	45	39	19	75	36	172	37	56	12	240	51
11	140	45	65	21	108	34	145	61	66	28	28	12
12	43	41	19	18	44	42	59	59	19	19	22	22
13	13	46	5	18	10	36	45	50	20	22	25	28
14	101	41	48	20	95	39	90	47	42	22	60	31
15	65	48	23	17	48	35	56	46	11	9	56	46
16	67	69	30	31	0	0	43	45	21	22	32	33
17	65	47	36	26	37	27	98	56	46	26	30	17
18	101	53	46	24	44	23	48	48	21	21	31	31
20	16	70	5	22	2	9	23	66	8	23	4	11
21	56	42	24	18	54	40	128	52	70	28	48	20
22	19	83	4	17	0	0	72	43	39	23	56	34
23	44	34	17	13	67	52	54	30	22	12	102	57
30	25	69	11	31	0	0	82	43	30	16	81	42
31	43	33	17	13	70	54	108	44	52	21	85	35
32	135	43	47	15	132	42	79	34	36	16	115	50
33	42	57	12	16	20	27	88	57	39	25	28	18
34	66	52	28	22	34	27	40	71	16	29	0	0
36	33	56	13	22	13	22	113	61	40	22	33	18
37	63	41	29	19	60	40	30	41	16	22	28	38
39	70	69	29	29	2	2	218	52	106	25	97	23
43	85	32	38	14	146	54	77	19	39	11	279	71
44	95	57	32	19	39	24	44	47	18	19	32	34
Mean	64	47	27	20	45	33	80	47	35	20	66	32
Median	63	48	24	19	39	30	77	47	30	22	34	31

Table 3.5

Number and Percentage of C, CA, and CAC+
Summary Statistics for Men and Women

	Ego Male (N=29)		Ego Female (N=29)		Both Egos (N=58)	
	N	%	N	%	N	%
C						
Mean	64	47	80	47	72	49
Median	63	48	77	47	64.5	47
Range	13-140		23-218		13-218	
CA						
Mean	27	20	35	20	31	21
Median	24	19	30	22	28	21
Range	4-65		8-106		4-106	
CAC+						
Mean	45	33	66	32	56	30
Median	39	30	34	31	38	31
Range	0-146		0-279		0-279	

Do these husband-wife differences have any significance? Or are they--as they could easily be--a function of chance variation in samples as small as ours? Table 3.7 shows that the latter is indeed the case.

Finally, when our families are broken down into the three age-groups, none of these groups tends significantly to exceed the probability levels shown in table 3.7, as table 3.8 shows.

Age, however, does have some effect on the distribution of the percentages of C, CA, and CAC+ kin. Table 3.9 gives the mean percentages for the three kin categories for the three age-groups. Increasing age in our male informants reduces the proportion of con-sanguineals and increases the proportion of CAC+. Table 3.10 shows that this trend is not statistically significant for women. The same change is noted between young and middle-aged informants. However, the trend is reversed in the kin universes of older female infor-mants.

Finally, our clearest findings about the distribution of %C, %CA, and %CAC+ are obtained when their relation to total genealogy size is considered. For both male and female informants, %C and %CA

Table 3.6

Percentage of the Total Genealogy Which
Is C, CA, CAC+, by Sex Group

%	Ego Male			Ego Female		
	C	CA	CAC+	C	CA	CAC+
0–5			4			2
6–10			2		3	
11–15		5	2		4	2
16–20		11		1	4	5
21–25		6	3		12	3
26–30		4	4	2	5	1
31–35	4	3	3	3		6
36–40			5	1	1	1
41–45	7		2	5		1
46–50	4			5		2
51–55	3		4	4		2
56–60	6			3		3
61–65				3		
66–70	4			1		
71–75				1		1
76–80						
81–85	1					

Table 3.7

Significance Levels for Differences in %C, %CA, %CAC+
between Husbands and Wives
(Wilcoxen Matched Pairs Signed Rank Test)

%C	%CA	%CAC+
p=.16	p=.45	p=.16
H>W	H>W	W>H

correlate negatively with kin universe size, and %CAC+ correlates
positively. For both men and women, the correlation with genealogy
size is stronger for %C than for %CA. For all three percentages,
the trends are stronger for men than for women. Table 3.11 presents
these correlations with their significance levels.

Table 3.8

Significance Levels for Differences in %C, %CA, %CAC+
between Husbands and Wives for Three Age-Groups
(Wilcoxen Matched Pairs Signed Rank Test)

	Young	Middle	Old
%C	p=.38, H>W	p=.13, H>W	p=.39, H>W
%CA	p=.22, H>W	p=.46, W>H	p=.39, W>H
%CAC+	p=.25, W>H	p=.18, W>H	p=.44, H>W

Table 3.9

Mean Percentage C, CA, CAC+

	Young		*Middle*		*Old*	
	Ego H	Ego W	Ego H	Ego W	Ego H	Ego W
C	54.1	51.7	50.8	44.3	47.0	45.9
CA	22.0	19.4	18.8	19.5	22.0	22.8
CAC+	23.9	28.8	30.4	36.2	31.0	31.3

Table 3.10

Correlation of %C, %CA, and %CAC+ with Age of Informant
(Spearman Rank Correlation)

	Ego Male	Ego Female
%C	$r_S = -.3144$ $p<.05$	$r_S = -.05$ NS
%CA	$r_S = -.115$ NS	$r_S = .293$ $p<.10$
%CAC+	$r_S = .294$ $p<.10$	$r_S = -.03$ NS

Table 3.11

Correlation of %C, %CA, and %CAC+
with Total Genealogy Size

	Ego Male	Ego Female
%C	$r_S = -.54$ p<.005	$r_S = -.39$ p<.025
%CA	$r_S = -.27$ p<.10	$r_S = -.25$ NS
%CAC+	$r_S = .51$ p<.025	$r_S = .32$ p<.05

Table 3.12 presents the mean percentage of consanguineals
and the spouses of consanguineals in various sizes of kin universes.
While there is some variation in the middle-range sizes, the smallest universes have the lowest proportion and the largest the highest
proportion of CAC+. The proportion of CA seems to remain about the
same for all sizes.

Table 3.12

Average %C and %CAC+ and Size of the Kin Universe

Size of Kin Universe	*Ego Male*		*Ego Female*	
	%C	%CAC+	%C	%CAC+
0-50 . .	67.0	11.1	65.7	11.4
51-100 . .	56.8	18.7	46.9	26.2
101-150 . .	44.2	37.1	46.0	34.4
151-200 . .	52.6	25.3	46.7	32.6
201+ . . .	41.2	41.1	41.5	39.9

Thus far, we have dealt with the percentage distribution of
the C, CA, and CAC+ categories. The raw figures themselves are interesting. The means, medians, and the ranges for male and female
Egos and for both Egos combined for the raw number of C, CA, and CAC+
were given in table 3.5. When those figures are broken down by age,

the dominant pattern is for the young male Ego to know the fewest in
each category (C, CA, or CAC+), the young female Ego to know slightly
more, the middle-aged male Ego to know still more, and so forth.
Table 3.13 presents these figures.

Table 3.13

Number of Relatives by Age, Sex, and Category

	Young		*Middle*		*Old*	
	Ego Male (N=10)	Ego Female (N=10)	Ego Male (N=11)	Ego Female (N=11)	Ego Male (N=8)	Ego Female (N=8)
C						
Mean	45	62	68	74	80	96
Median . . .	38	50	44	72	77	94
CA						
Mean	18	23	27	33	38	51
Median . . .	16	19	18	28	37	44
CAC+						
Mean	22	38	53	59	61	98
Median . . .	16	30	60	56	56	54

Both tables 3.5 and 3.13 suggest that, in all three categories, women know more kin than their husbands. This is confirmed by
a Wilcoxen test. The probability levels are presented in table 3.14.

Table 3.14

Significance Levels for Differences in Raw C, CA, and CAC+
Scores between Husbands and Wives

C (N=40)	CA (N=38)	CAC+ (N=28)
p=.0055	p=.0192	p=.0694

Table 3.15 shows the probability levels for wives' knowing
more of the three categories of kin in the three age-groups. Note
that the tendencies are strongest in the young category for all three
types of kin.

Table 3.15

Significance Levels for Differences in Raw C, CA, and CAC+
Scores between Husbands and Wives for the Three Age-Groups

	Young	Middle	Old
C	.0516	.1469	.0764
CA	.0668	.1271	.2206
CAC+	.1210	.1762	.3372

Finally, when the raw scores for the three kin categories
are correlated with the age of the informant, we see that the correlations are quite high for male and female informants for the CA category. The number of C kin known tends to increase with age for female informants but not for males. However, the number of CAC+ kin
tends to increase with age for male informants but not for females.
Table 3.16 gives the correlation coefficients and their associated
probability levels.

Table 3.16

Correlation of Age with Raw Number of C, CA, and CAC+
Kin Known by Male and Female Informants

	Ego Male	Ego Female
C (N=40)	$r_S = .11$ NS	$r_S = .2623$ p<.10
CA (N=40)	$r_S = .35$ p<.025	$r_S = .57$ p<.01
CAC+ (N=29)	$r_S = .40$ p<.025	$r_S = .23$ NS

Thus, when age and genealogy size are considered together,
there seem to be distinct differences between men and women. While
older informants have larger kin universes than younger ones, men and
women differ in the way the composition of their universes changes.
Men, as they grow older, seem to increase the number of CA and CAC+
that they report. This increase lowers the proportion of consan-

guineals and increases the proportion of CAC+, while the increase in
the number of consanguineals is just sufficient to leave the proportion of that group unchanged in the total. Women, on the other hand,
show an increase in the absolute number of C and CA, while the number
of CAC+ does not correlate with age. This leaves the proportion of
C and CAC+ more or less unchanged while the proportion of CA increases. Of course, it is not necessarily proper to speak of these
differences as changes which are due to growing older. These data
may merely reflect a difference in the pattern of the older generation compared to that of the younger.

In sum, the kin universes of our informants tend to be divisible into the three categories C, CA, and CAC+ in the proportion
5:2:3, although there is great variety. These proportions seem about
equally consistent for husbands and wives. Older informants may tend
to know more CAC+ and less C than younger informants, both by absolute number and by percentage of genealogy. Informants with larger
kin universes have higher proportions of CAC+. Within each category,
wives seem to know more people than their husbands.

III. Generation and Collateral Removal

We know examine the distribution of consanguineal relatives across
the dimensions of generation and collateral removal. We shall present two estimates of the number of relatives who probably exist and
compare them with the number and location of relatives actually reported.

Ego and his siblings belong to the same generation. Ego's
parents and their siblings are one generation "above" Ego, while
Ego's children and his siblings' children are one generation "below."
Following conventional formal analytic notation, we shall designate
Ego's generation G^0, the parental generation G^{+1}, the generation of
Ego's children G^{-1}, and so on.

In the same way, collateral removal can be designated by the
letter R. Ego, his parents, and his children are all of Ego's own
line, and this line is designated R^0. Ego's siblings, his parents'
siblings, and his grandparents' siblings are all removed from Ego's
line by one degree and are designated R^1. In turn, their cousins are
removed by two degrees, designated R^2, and so on.

Table 3.17 gives the common English terms for individuals in
each cell, defined by the coordination of these two dimensions.

The number of individuals in each cell can be predicted--al-
though with more precision for some cells than for others. Knowing
the accepted theories of biology, we expect each individual to have

Table 3.17

Table of Generation and Collateral Removal Showing
Common English Terms for Relatives in Each Cell

	R^0	R^1	R^2	R^3
G^{+2}	*Grandparents* MoMo, MoFa, FaMo, FaFa	*Great-aunts and Great-uncles* MoMoBr, MoMoSi, FaMoBr, FaMoSi, MoFaBr, MoFaSi, FaFaBr, FaFaSi	*Grandparents' 1st Cousins* FaFaFaBrCh, MoMoMoBrCh, etc.	*Grandparents' 2d Cousins* FaFaFaFaBrChCh, MoMoMoMoSiChCh, etc.
G^{+1}	*Parents* Mo, Fa	*Uncles, Aunts* MoBr, MoSi, FaBr, FaSi	*Parents' 1st Cousins* MoFaBrCh, MoMoBrCh, FaFaBrCh, FaFaSiCh, etc.	*Parents' 2d Cousins* FaFaFaBrChCh, MoMoMoBrChCh, etc.
G^0	EGO	*Siblings* Br, Si	*1st Cousins* MoSiCh, MoBrCh, FaSiCh, FaBrCh	*2d Cousins* MoFaBrChCh, MoMoBrChCh, FaFaBrChCh, etc.
G^{-1}	*Children* So, Da	*Nephews, Nieces* BrCh, SiCh	*1st Cousins' Children* MoSiSoCh, FaSiSoCh, FaBrSoCh, etc.	*2d Cousins' Children* MoFaBrChChCh, MoMoBrChChCh, FaFaBrChChCh, etc.
G^{-2}	*Grandchildren* SoSo, SoDa, DaSo, DaDa	*Siblings' Grandchildren* BrChCh, SiChCh	*1st Cousins' Grandchildren* MoSiSoChCh, FaSiSoChCh, FaBrSoChCh, etc.	*2d Cousins' Grandchildren* MoFaBrChChChCh, MoMoBrChChChCh, MoFaBrChChChCh, etc.

exactly two parents.[1] Thus, our 80 informants should report just
160 parents, 320 grandparents, 640 great-grandparents ($G^{+3}R^0$), and
so on. Further, if we had a random sample from a population known
to have an average of three children per family, we would expect 160
siblings (G^0R^1), 320 aunts and uncles ($G^{+1}R^1$), and so on.

Unfortunately, not knowing exactly what population our informants represent, we cannot use independent measures of family
size from sources like the national census. Instead, we construct
two plausible models for predicting cell size. The first is an ide-
al model that postulates constant sib-set size throughout the entire
universe. The second model uses actual ratios between cells that
are close to Ego to project the number of kin who may be expected to
exist in the cells distant from Ego.

For our first model, we shall assume that each family will
have had exactly three children. Thus, for each informant, there
are four grandparents, and each of these has just two siblings, being eight great- aunts and uncles. These eight people have twenty-
four offspring, the parents' first cousins ($G^{+1}R^2$). Each of the two
parents has two siblings, being four aunts and uncles. The cell
frequencies predicted by this model for all cells are given in table
3.18. However, each figure has been multiplied by eighty--the number of informants.

For the second model, turn again to table 3.18 and note that
it lists the total number of individuals in each cell who were actually reported. We start with 80 informants who have 160 parents
and 222 siblings. This means that the 80 pairs of parents had 222
+ 80 = 302 children, or an average of 3.77 children per couple. In
this fashion we generate table 3.19.

There are many important points in table 3.19. For the moment, however, suffice it to say that the figures in the R^0 column
can be used in place of the constant three to generate the third set
of figures on table 3.18. Since the figure 1.98 seems quite low,
probably because information has been lost through time in the mem-
ories of informants and their ancestors, we have arbitrarily pro-
jected the five from G^{+2} back through G^{+3}. We have also taken the
liberty of rounding these figures to one digit for our calculations.

We now have two estimates of the size of the potential kin
universe to compare with the measured size of the known kin universe.
The first is likely to be a low estimate, while we suspect the second
model is too high. By simply dividing the expected by the observed,
we obtain the percentage of relatives known, given in table 3.20.

The first conclusion to be drawn from these data is obvious.

Table 3.18

Number of Consanguineal Relatives by Generation
and Collateral Removal*

	R^0		R^1		R^2		R^3	
G^{+2}		320		640		3,840		23,040
	292	320	312	1,280	24	12,800	1	
G^{+1}		160		320		1,920		11,520
	160	160	647	640	410	6,400	20	64,000
G^0		80		160		960		5,760
	80	80	222	240	1,040	2,560	348	256,000
G^{-1}		120		480		2,880		17,280
	118	120	445	720	1,154	7,680	165	768,000
G^{-2}		360		1,440		8,640		51,840
	30		137		216		15	

*Key:

	Est. model 1
Reported	Est. model 2

Table 3.19

Mean Number of Children per Couple
Based on Consanguineal Ratios

	R^0	R^1	R^2	R^3
G^{+3}	1.98			
G^{+2}	5.04	1.31		
G^{+1}	3.77	1.60	0.85	
G^0	2.95	2.00	1.11	0.47
G^{-1}	0.24	0.34	0.18	0.09

45

Table 3.20

Percentage of Expected Relatives Reported
by Generation and Collateral Removal*

	R^0	R^1	R^2	R^3
G^{+2}	91%	49%	0%	
	91	24	0	
G^{+1}	100	202	21	0%
	100	101	6	0
G^0	100	139	101	6
	100	92	41	0
G^{-1}	98	93	40	1
	98	62	15	0

*Key:

Reported/est. model 1
Reported/est. model 2

There is a remarkable amount of loss evident in the reported figures, even in cells that may be considered close to Ego. Further, there are three notable aspects of the pattern of loss. First, relatives located within two squares of Ego are almost completely reported. Second, relatives located about three cells distant from Ego show a "fading out." A substantial number of people are indeed reported, but most are not. Third, beyond this rather fuzzy boundary there is a precipitous drop; the percentage of relatives reported drops to almost none.

These conclusions are also evident in the figures in table 3.19. Notice that, from grandparents to Ego, the mean number of children drops from five through four to three. This is consistent with the recognized delcine in birth rates in America during the last fifty years. The figure for great-grandparents, however, seems to suffer from the partial loss associated with being located on the boundary we have noted.

We have glossed over a number of weak points in this analysis in order to arrive at our cautious conclusions. First, we have perforce selected informants whose lineal ancestors *did* marry and have children. We have overestimated the number of potential kin by some function of the number of ancestors who did not reproduce. Second, by excluding those people to whom no link could be traced, we have undoubtedly biased our sample against distant relatives. Third, because our informants did include young couples whose children were not fully mature, not much can be inferred from the figures in the G^{-2} line.

In addition, some of our informants provided information from their family histories that explains some of the loss of information. A few knew that uncles or aunts remained "in the old country" but had lost touch. A few others (mostly Jewish) reported that whole branches of their family were disrupted or killed by the Nazis during World War II and that nothing had been heard of them since. Finally, several reported family disputes of such magnitude that members of their parental sib-set simply ceased communicating.

We have already discovered that our female informants reported more consanguineals than their husbands. Table 3.21 shows where these additional people are located along the dimensions of generation and collateral removal.

Table 3.21

Number of Consanguineal Relatives by Generation,
Collateral Removal, and Sex of Informant

	R^0		R^1		R^2		R^3	
	Ego Male	Ego Female	Ego Male	Ego Female	Ego Male	Ego Female	Ego Male	Ego Female
G^{+2}	143	149	116	196	5	19	1	0
G^{+1}	80	80	323	324	129	281	6	14
G^0	EGO	EGO	102	120	485	555	121	227
G^{-1}			221	224	548	606	50	115
G^{-2}			84	53	87	129	0	15

Clearly, while men and women know about the same number of people in the cells within about two cells of Ego, in the more distant cells the totals for women far exceed those for men. However, this may merely indicate that women are more certain of the genealogical links to their distant relations and/or that they had twice as many opportunities to report them.

Tables 3.22 and 3.23 break down the preceding table by the

47

Table 3.22

Number of Consanguineals Reported by Men by Generation and Collateral Removal of Alter and Age of Informant

		R^0	R^1	R^2	R^3	R^4	R^5
	O						
G^{+4}	M						
	Y	4					
	O	4	2				
G^{+3}	M	12					
	Y	21	2				
	O	47	23				
G^{+2}	M	46	34		1		
	Y	50	59	5			
	O	25	137	30			
G^{+1}	M	27	110	37			
	Y	28	76	62	6		
	O		47	198	22		
G^0	M		34	179	32		
	Y		31	108	67	14	
	O		85	195	23		
G^{-1}	M		74	224	19	1	
	Y		62	129	8		3
	O		71	62			
G^{-2}	M		13	14			
	Y			11			
	O		3				
G^{-3}	M						
	Y						

Table 3.23

Number of Consanguineals Reported by Women
by Generation and Collateral Removal
of Alter and Age of Informant

		R^0	R^1	R^2	R^3	R^4
G^{+4}	O	2				
	M					
	Y	2				
G^{+3}	O	18	4			
	M	30				
	Y	37	7			
G^{+2}	O	46	59	18		
	M	46	40			
	Y	57	97	1		
G^{+1}	O	26	114	95	14	
	M	26	98	98		
	Y	28	112	88		
G^0	O		54	210	50	8
	M		42	132	91	
	Y		24	213	86	
G^{-1}	O	32	107	256	62	
	M	33	75	181	37	
	Y	40	42	169	16	
G^{-2}	O	29	30	71	15	
	M		23	57		
	Y			1		
G^{-3}	O			2		
	M					
	Y					

three age-groups of informants. In general, older informants reported more of their junior relatives, while the younger informants reported more relatives in the generations senior to themselves. This
would seem reasonable, since the older informants allowed more time
for their generational equals (some of whom may have been their chron-
ological juniors) to reproduce and raise families. The loss of the
elders to the older informants can be partially explained by two factors. More of them were likely to have died than were the equivalent
relatives of younger informants, and dead people in general seem to
go unreported (see section on "Death" below). Second, this loss may
represent branches of the family who were lost in some way--e.g.,
being left behind in the old country. One distinct aberration is
the $G^{+1}R^1$ square, particularly as reported by men, where the pattern
is clearly reversed.

To reiterate: relatives who are genealogically close (within
one or two cells) to Ego are almost completely reported. Those who
are far (more than three cells) from Ego are almost completely lost.
Those who lie along the indefinite boundary between close and far
are only partially reported. While men and women seem to know about
the same number of close relatives, women know more relatives in the
intermediate and distant squares.

IV. *Links*

We now turn our attention to the links--the persons through whom genealogical ties are traced. First we consider the general question
of mother's side versus father's side and then investigate the general patterns of links through consanguinity and affinity.

a. *Mother's Side, Father's Side*

It is not unusual for American informants to compare or contrast
what they call "mother's side of the family" with "father's side of
the family." Sometimes this distinction is made in terms of the fact
that the two sides do not get along, or that they do get along, or
in another form. But it seemed worth asking whether family side
makes any difference in the content of the kin universe.

Pooling all the material from our informants, we find that
there are about 400 more persons reported for mother's side than for
father's side out of some 7,000 persons used for this analysis. This
means that about 5% more persons are reported for mother's side than
father's side.

But table 3.24 shows that this difference is located almost
entirely with the mother's side of female informants' families. Male
informants report about as many persons on mother's side as on father's side.

Table 3.24

Side of Family by Sex of Ego*

	Ego Male	Ego Female	Total
Father's . .	1,545	1,826	3,371
Mother's . .	1,555	2,238	3,793
Total	3,100	4,064	7,164

* Includes C, CA, and R^2 but no others.

We already know that the larger size of the woman informant's kin universe is located primarily among distant kin rather than close kin. If women report more relatives on the mother's side than on the father's side, while men report about equal numbers, it is reasonable to assume that the larger numbers of kin reported by women are distant relatives on the mother's side.

Table 3.25 suggests that this may indeed be so. The question is simply whether the genealogy contains one or more relatives more distant than the grandparents. Table 3.25 indicates that a much higher proportion of our female informants' genealogies reported such distant kin.

Table 3.25

One or More Distant Kin beyond Grandparents
Reported by Male and Female Ego
(N=84)

	One or More beyond Grandparents	No One beyond Grandparents
Ego Male	26	14
Ego Female . . .	36	8

We see that thirty-six genealogies of female informants report distant kin beyond grandparents, while only eight do not. Is there a perceptible bias toward distant kin on the mother's side for women? Table 3.26 shows the mean number of distant kin (more distant than grandparents) for the forty husband-wife pairs of genealogies. Clearly, women report a higher mean number of distant kin on

the mother's side of the family than the father's side. Table 3.26
shows another thing that table 3.25 did not enable us to perceive--
the mean number of distant relatives for male Ego is higher on the
father's side than on the mother's side.

Table 3.26

Mean Number of Distant Kin, Mother's Side,
Father's Side, by Sex of Ego
(N=80)

	Father's Side	Mother's Side
Ego Male	8.2	4.1
Ego Female . . .	8.9	15.6

These results are statistically significant at the .01 level
for female Egos and approach the .05 level for male Egos.

Obviously, mother's side of the family can be approached
through mother's mother as well as mother's father, while father's
side can be reached through father's mother as well as father's father. Is there any bias evident for any one of the grandparents?
Table 3.27 shows the mean number of distant kin through each grandparent. It demonstrates that, although the bias of female informants
for distant kin through the mother's side of the family remains,
there is no bias toward one or the other grandparent. But there is
a tendency for distant kin to be linked more through father's father
than father's mother on the father's side for both male and female
informants.

Table 3.27

Mean Number of Distant Kin Known through
FF, FM, MM, and MF by Sex of Ego
(N=80)

	FF	FM	MF	MM
Ego Male	5.0	3.2	1.3	2.8
Ego Female . . .	5.3	3.6	7.9	7.7

b. Consanguinity and Affinity

Let us examine how relatives are linked to Ego. There are, of course,
two kinds of links that define kinship in American culture: blood
and marriage.

First we shall consider the number of consanguineals reported
according to the sex of the informant, the sex of the first link, and
the sex of the last consanguineal in the chain. Then we shall examine the number of affinals (CA and CAC+) according to the generation
and degree of collateral removal of their linking consanguineal, the
sex of the informant, the sex of the consanguineal link, and the sex
of Alter.

Consanguineals

Table 3.28 gives the number of consanguineals according to these criteria.

Table 3.28

Number of Consanguineals by Sex of Informant,
Sex of Link, and Sex of Relative

Link	Alter			
	Male	Female	Sex Unknown	Total
Male Informant				
Father, Brother . .	614	524	148	1,286
Mother, Sister . .	520	598	164	1,282
Total	1,134	1,122		
Female Informant				
Father, Brother . .	707	555	195	1,457
Mother, Sister . .	730	836	200	1,766
Total	1,437	1,391		

It would seem from this evidence that knowledge of consanguineals is biased slightly toward greater knowledge of those whose links
are between members of the same sex than of the opposite sex. While
men know as many men as women, and as many through mother and sister
as through father and brother, they seem to know more men through
father and brother and more women through mother and sister. Similarly, despite the fact that women know more consanguineals through
mother and sister than through father and brother, within each group

they tend to know more relatives of the same sex as the link than of the opposite sex as the link.

CA, CAC+

Tables 3.29 and 3.30 show the distribution of CAs and CAC+s by the generation and degree of collateral removal of the consanguineal through whom they are linked. Clearly, this distribution parallels

Table 3.29

Number of C, CA, and CAC+ by Generation
and Collateral Removal

		R^0	R^1	*Wife* R^2	R^3	R^4
G^{+4}	C	4				
	CA					
	CAC+					
G^{+3}	C	85	11			
	CA		5			
	CAC+					
G^{+2}	C	149	196	19		
	CA		151	8		
	CAC+		41	1		
G^{+1}	C	80	324	281	14	
	CA		269	193	5	
	CAC+		617	40		
G^0	C		120	555	227	8
	CA		106	367	84	
	CAC+		1,019	216	54	
G^{-1}	C	105	224	606	115	
	CA	16	35	105	8	
	CAC+	235	156	24		
G^{-2}	C	29	53	129	15	
	CA		1	13		
	CAC+		2	2		

Table 3.30

Number of C, CA, and CAC+ by Generation
and Collateral Removal

		R^0	R^1	Husband R^2	R^3	R^4	R^5
G^{+4}	C	4					
	CA						
	CAC+						
G^{+3}	C	37	4				
	CA		2				
	CAC+						
G^{+2}	C	143	116	5	1		
	CA		80	5			
	CAC+		10				
G^{+1}	C	80	323	129	6		
	CA		233	106	6		
	CAC+		369	22			
G^0	C		102	485	121	14	
	CA		90	380	33	3	
	CAC+		656	217	4	1	
G^{-1}	C		221	548	50	1	3
	CA		57	79	1		
	CAC+		69	62	2		
G^{-2}	C		84	87			
	CA		6				
	CAC+		8				

closely the distribution of consanguineals discussed in section III
above. It exhibits the same high numbers within a distance of two
cells from Ego and the same fuzzy boundary followed by a drop almost
to zero.

Indeed, the pattern for the CAC+s is striking. Almost all
are brought in through consanguineals who are quite closely related

to Ego--siblings, children, aunts, uncles, and first cousins. It is
not surprising, since women tend to report more of their distant
relatives than men do, that women report some thirteen times as many
CAC+ through their second cousins as male informants do. It is peculiar that men report three times as many CAC+ through their first
cousins' children as women do. If one considers the number of CAC+
brought in by each CA (CAC+/CA), one notes that this ratio is less
than one for all but the closest four squares and reaches a maximum
of almost fifteen CAC+ brought in by each child-in-law.

V. Death

In principle, Americans may trace their ancestors without limit into
the past. Indeed, informants sometimes remarked "We are all relatives because we are all descended from Adam and Eve." But, as we
have seen, our informants tended to limit themselves to a few proxi-
mate generations--which is as far back as their knowledge carried
them.

The further an ascendant generation is from Ego, the higher
the proportion of persons in that generation we can expect to be
dead at the time we collect Ego's genealogy. If an informant actually knows of everyone in each ascendant generation, even if he
goes back only two or three generations, we can expect a substantial
part of his kin universe to be dead. Our informants reported as indicated in table 3.31.

Table 3.31

Percentage of Kin Universe Alive

% Alive	Number of Genealogies
50-60	4
61-70	8
71-80	37
81-90	33
91-100	2

Mean percentage of live relatives: males, 78.1; females, 79.2.

One might expect that older people, having lived longer and
seen others die and having known many relatives who had died, would
provide genealogies containing a higher proportion of dead persons
than younger informants. This was not true for our informants, as
table 3.32 shows.

Table 3.32

Percentage of Living Consanguineals
by Age and Sex of Informant
(29 H/W pairs)

	Husband	Wife
Young	77.9%	77.5%
Middle	80.2	80.5
Old	74.1	77.0

From these figures, one is led to believe that dead relatives
are somehow less important than live ones. It seems that dead relatives are quickly forgotten.

Tables 3.33 and 3.34 detail the percentage of consanguineals
in each category of generation and collateral removal who are reported
as alive, according to the age and sex of informants. These tables
show that, in the close senior locations (parents, grandparents,
aunts, and uncles), the older informants report more dead relatives.
These are also the cells where the fewest relatives seem to go unreported. (See "Generation and Collateral Removal," above.) Furthermore, as could be expected, the higher the ascendant generation, the
more reported relatives are dead when the genealogy is collected.
And, as one moves outward within a generation (from R^1 to R^2 and then
to R^3), in general the fewer relatives are reported who are dead.
This seems to indicate that distant dead relatives are somehow less
"important" than close ones and therefore less likely to be reported.
Some support for this point is found in table 3.35. It should be
remembered that these categories usually contain the smallest number
of people.

To measure more accurately the importance of dead relatives,
we asked our informants for the dates of death. We assumed that people would be more likely to note and remember the death dates for
relatives more important to them than for those less important to
them.

In addition, we wondered whether the directness of the genealogical tie would affect the importance of a dead relative. Our
information on this is presented in table 3.36.

When we look at the percentage of live relatives in each category, it seems that dead CAC+ relatives are indeed less important

Table 3.33

Percentage of Relatives Reported Alive
by Generation, Degree of Collateral
Removal, Age and Sex of Informant

| | | R^0 | | R^1 | | R^2 | | R^3 | |
		Male	Female	Male	Female	Male	Female	Male	Female
	O	4%	18%	39%	28%				
G^{+2}	M	0	13	17	39				
	Y	0	4	13	24				
	O	89	76	61	68	92%	92%		
G^{+1}	M	56	65	53	41	84	89		
	Y	32	27	25	24	37	80		
	O			87	96	94	97	96%	92%
G^0	M			91	76	96	93	91	98
	Y			76	89	87	84	96	96
	O			97	98	99	100	*	*
G^{-1}	M			99	100	100	99	*	100
	Y			98	99	99	97	100	100
	O			*	*	*	*	*	*
G^{-2}	M			*	100	*	95	*	*
	Y			100	96	100	97	*	*

* N=Less than 20.

Table 3.34

Percentage of Consanguineals Reported Alive
by Generation and Collateral Removal

| | R^0 | | R^1 | | R^2 | | R^3 | |
	Ego Male	Ego Female	Ego Male	Ego Female	Ego Male	Ego Female	Ego Male	Ego Female
G^{+2}	2%	12%	28%	30%				
G^{+1}	60	55	42	44	77%	86%		
G^0			84	92	92	91	94%	96%
G^{-1}			98	99	99	99	98	99

58

Table 3.35

Percentage of All Dead Consanguineal Kin
Found in Selected Categories

	Ego Male	Ego Female
Grandparents . .	23.7%	17.9%
Parents	5.5	5.2
Aunts, uncles .	31.5	24.6
Total	60.7	47.7
All other . . .	39.3	52.3

Table 3.36

Date of Death by C, CA, and CAC+*

Date of Death	C Men	C Women	CA Men	CA Women	CAC+ Men	CAC+ Women
Known exactly .	7.6%	6.5%	6.6%	4.7%	2.8%	2.5%
	(196)	(229)	(72)	(71)	(40)	(61)
Estimated . . .	4.9	4.7	5.0	4.3	3.1	3.0
	(126)	(166)	(55)	(64)	(44)	(73)
Unknown	9.1	9.4	9.8	11.3	10.9	8.8
	(235)	(328)	(107)	(170)	(154)	(211)
Alive	77.2	76.9	77.4	77.3	81.0	84.1
	(1,989)	(2,693)	(848)	(1,160)	(1,150)	(2,023)
Not asked . . .	1.2	2.4	1.3	2.3	2.2	1.6
	(31)	(85)	(14)	(35)	(31)	(38)
Total	100.0%	100.0%	100.0%	100.0%	100.0%	100.0%
Number of Informants .	40	44	40	44	40	44

* Does not include children or relatives related through children.

than dead consanguineals. At least, fewer of them appear to be reported. However, the dead spouses of consanguinals are reported as fully as dead consanguineals.

When we determine whether date of death is known at least approximately, the pattern becomes clearer. Informants could at least estimate dates of death for 717 of 1,280 (56%) consanguineals but for only 262 of 539 (49%) CAs. CAC+s were even more poorly remembered, with dates of death known or estimated for only 218 of 583 (27%).

Table 3.36 also suggests that women are less concerned with the memory of dead CAs and CAC+s than men, but the differences are very slight.

In sum, more than three-quarters of those persons reported on the genealogies were alive, fewer than one-quarter were dead. This is true whatever the informant's age, so that even the older informants, who might have reported a higher proportion dead, did not. The dates of death were unknown for just under half of the instances. The dead were certainly underreported for the ascending generations--the more so the greater the genealogical distance from Ego--but they also seem to have been underreported for even the generations closest to Ego's. And the fact that the dates of death were either unknown or had to be estimated for most of those reported dead is consistent with the remark which informants frequently made when they replied to the opening question, "List for me all those whom you consider to be your relatives." They asked whether the dead should be included: "Do you want the dead ones too?" or "He's dead. Should I include the dead ones?" The dead seem to occupy an uncertain place in the kin universe.

VI. *First Names*

We have said that knowing that a relative is dead is having one piece of information about him, while knowing the date of his death is having even more knowledge.

By the same token, knowing that a person exists as a part of a kin universe is one thing; knowing his first name is something more. Thus, an informant knows that his parents had parents of their own; however, the informant who can report the names of all four grandparents is telling us more.[2]

One piece of information which may be considered a prerequisite to knowing Alter's first name is knowing Alter's sex. Table 3.37 presents the percentage of persons in each generational and collateral removal location whose sex is unknown. The proportion of "neuters" increases steadily with generational distance below Ego. One would also expect the proportion of infants and young children, whose sex would probably not be very important to Ego, would follow the same pattern. However, within these generations, the percentage of persons whose sex is unknown increases directly and also directly with increased degree of collateral removal. This may indicate that increased genealogical distance may decrease the importance of relatives.

Table 3.37

Percentage of Sex Unknown by Generation and
Collateral Removal by Sex of Informant

	R^0		R^1		R^2		R^3	
	Male	Female	Male	Female	Male	Female	Male	Female
G^{+3}	0%	0%	*	*				
G^{+2}	0	0	3%	1%	*	*		
G^{+1}	0	0	8	7	2%	9%	*	*
G^0			0	0	4	3	21%	18%
G^{-1}			1	0	28	21	46	64
G^{-2}			11	4	51	51	*	*

* N=Less than 20.

Returning to the consideration of first names, we present our data in tables 3.38-3.41. Tables 3.38 and 3.39 indicate that knowledge of Alter's first name followed the same patterns as knowledge of Alter's date of death. The first names of consanguineals were known slightly more often than the names of their spouses, while the names of CAC+s were known about half as often. Once again, the informant's age seems to have little importance. Middle-aged people may remember more names, but this is not clearly significant.

Tables 3.40 and 3.41 put these data into greater perspective.

First, although the percentages in each category are higher for female Ego than for male Ego in all but two cases, the percentage differences do not seem very large, except for the grandparental category ($G^{+2}R^0$, 20% difference), great-aunt and great-uncle category ($G^{+2}R^1$, 14% difference), the grand-nephew and grand-niece category ($G^{-2}R^1$, 31% difference), and the second cousin category (G^0R^3, 11% difference).

Second, our informants knew a large number of great-aunts'

Table 3.38

First Names*

	C		CA		CAC+	
	Men	Women	Men	Women	Men	Women
Known	65.0%	67.6%	56.9%	57.6%	31.3%	32.9%
	(1,674)	(2,367)	(624)	(864)	(442)	(793)
Unknown	32.6	29.8	41.4	39.3	65.9	64.4
	(840)	(1,044)	(454)	(590)	(939)	(1,551)
Not asked . . .	2.4	2.7	1.7	3.1	3.0	2.6
	(63)	(93)	(19)	(46)	(43)	(63)

* Does not include children or those related through children.
N=40 men, 44 women.

and great-uncles' first names--82% and 83% respectively. Since the
most common form of address for aunts, uncles, great-aunts, and
great-uncles is the combination kinship term plus first name (Uncle
John, Aunt Mary), this may not be so surprising. But it is interesting to compare this category with its reciprocal, $G^{-1}R^2$, first
cousins' children; only 44% and 48% of the first names of these are
known. Here first name alone is the most common form of address.
These persons were not often known and even when they were, their
names were not often known. But with the senior generation, if the
persons were known, their names were almost always known.
    If we ask the same questions of the spouses of the consan-
guineals, fewer names of CA are known as distance increases, both

Table 3.39

Percentage of First Names Known

	C		CA	
	Male	Female	Male	Female
Young . . .	63.5%	69.1%	55.6%	61.6%
Middle . .	70.8	68.0	64.4	63.1
Old	65.8	73.2	54.3	55.9

N=40 men, 40 women.

Table 3.40

Percentage of First Name Known for Each Category
by Sex of Informant, Generation, and Degree
of Collateral Removal (Consanguineals Only)

| | R^0 | | R^1 | | R^2 | | R^3 | |
	Ego Male	Ego Female	Ego Male	Ego Female	Ego Male	Ego Female	Ego Male	Ego Female
G^{+2}	65%	85%	57%	71%	*	*	*	*
G^{+1}	100	100	82	90	82%	80%	*	*
G^0	Ego		99	100	84	86	36%	47%
G^{-1}			94	96	44	48	18	13
G^{-2}			45	76	11	22	*	*

* N=Less than 50.

Table 3.41

Percentage of First Name Known for Each Category by Sex
of Informant, Generation, Collateral Removal
(Spouses of Consanguineals [CA] Only)

| | R^1 | | R^2 | | R^3 | |
	Ego Male	Ego Female	Ego Male	Ego Female	Ego Male	Ego Female
G^{+2}	28%	35%	*	*	*	*
G^{+1}	82	85	50%	47%	*	*
G^0	98	98	51	61	*	*
G^{-1}	64	87	32	31	*	*
G^{-2}	*	*	*	*	*	*

* N=Less than 50.

for male and female informants. And again, female Egos have slightly higher percentages than male Egos. However, the differences seem trivial--with the possible exception of $G^{-1}R^1$, the spouses of nephews and nieces.

It is interesting to compare the percentages for some of the categories of consanguineals with those for their spouses. Take $G^{+1}R^1$, uncles and aunts, for instance. The percentages are almost the same: 82% and 82%, and 90% and 85%. This simply means that the first names of the husbands and wives of uncles and aunts were known as often as the first names of the uncles and aunts themselves. This is true for only one other category, namely, the sibling category (G^0R^1). The reciprocal of the uncle-aunt category is quite different in this respect. Although the names of 94% and 96% of the nephews and nieces ($G^{-1}R^1$) were known by male and female informants respectively, only 64% and 87% of the names of their spouses were known to male and female informants respectively. This seems consistent with the view that the nepotic relationship is by no means symmetrical with regard to the aunt or uncle by marriage, or the nephew or niece by marriage. The first names of aunts and uncles by marriage (the spouses of the uncles and aunts) were known as frequently as the first names of the aunts and uncles by blood, while the first names of the nephews and nieces were known more often than the first names of their spouses (Schneider 1965:300; 1968:82-83).

We have found here the usual and by now expected difference between male and female informants. Women seem to report more distant people on their genealogies, and they tend to know somewhat more first names than men. Yet, for both men and women, distance diminishes not only how many they report but also information they have about those they report, as measured by their knowledge of first names. And distance once again can be roughly measured as more than two squares from Ego; consanguineals are closest, CA next closest, and CAC+ most distant.

We can now again ask if the sex of Alter has any bearing on Ego's knowledge of Alter's first name. Do informants know women's first names more often than men's? Or do women know women's first names, men know men's first names and not know women's first names?

Reviewing the following tables, we see that there is a slight tendency, which is sometimes statistically significant, for persons to know more of the first names of those of the same sex as themselves. But on the whole, the sex of Alter is not very important, while the sex of Ego tends to be reflected in more names known. Everything else is constant. That is, for both male and female Egos, distance decreases the percentage of first names known, but for any given category at any given degree of distance, women tend to know more first names than men and so show a greater percentage of first names known than men. There is a slight tendency for women to know more women's names and men to know more men's names, but this does not seem to be significant in general.

We now turn to a somewhat different kind of knowledge of names. Here we ask a combination of questions. How much about his ancestry does an informant know, and how much does he know about these ancestors? Our measure here is, again, knowledge of names.

Table 3.42

Percentage Named by G and R and Sex of Alter,
Ego Female

	R^0 Alter		R^1 Alter		R^2 Alter		R^3 Alter	
	M	F	M	F	M	F	M	F
G^{+2}	85%	84%	61%	79%	*	*		
G^{+1}			97	97	86%	90%		
G^0			100	100	88	89	62%	51%
G^{-1}			97	94	58	60		
G^{-2}			72	82	37	41		

* N=Less than 50.

Table 3.43

Percentage Named by G and R and Sex of Alter,
Ego Male

	R^0 Alter		R^1 Alter		R^2 Alter		R^3 Alter	
	M	F	M	F	M	F	M	F
G^{+2}	68%	62%	62%	55%	*	*		
G^{+1}			90	89	87%	80%		
G^0			100	98	88	86	71%	43%
G^{-1}			97	93	59	60		
G^{-2}			61	30	33	5		

* N=Less than 50.

Table 3.44 indicates that a remarkably small proportion of
our informants knew the full names of their four grandparents, though
if we asked only if they knew any name, more of them knew something
about their grandparents than knew their full names. By "full names,"
we mean that a first and a last name were reported by the informant.
This means the informant knew his father's mother's first and maiden
name, his mother's mother's first and maiden name, his mother's father's first and last name, and his father's father's first name

(since the informant's last name is ordinarily the same as his father's father's). Thus seven of the eight (including father's father's last name) possible names were problematic and could not be
inferred directly by the informant.

Table 3.44

Number of Informants Knowing First, Last, or Full Name

	First or Last Name		Full Name	
	H	W	H	W
Parents only . .	5	2	5	2
1 of 4	5	0	13	1
2 of 4	11	2	7	13
3 of 4	6	7	7	9
4 of 4	14	32	9	18
Total	41	43	41	43

Table 3.44 shows that five of our male informants and two of
our female informants did not report the names of any of their grandparents. However, seventy-seven of our eighty-four informants reported at least one name for at least one grandparent.

Of those seventy-seven, however, only twenty-eight reported
at least one name for any direct ascendant beyond the grandparents.
Eighteen female and five male informants provided at least one name
for great-grandparents. Three female informants and two male informants provided at least one name for great-great-grandparents. Only
two of our informants (one man and one woman) went back further.

This leads us to our final point here. Men and women informants differ in the percentages of persons whose first names they
know. This suggests that perhaps, for example, women are closer to
and more interested in uncles and aunts than men and hence know the
first names of uncles and aunts more often than men. Or women may
have closer ties to women and hence know the first names of women
more often than men do. Or women may be more concerned with children
and younger people and so know the names of persons in the G^{-1} and
G^{-2} categories more often than men. Or men, since they are more involved with older people, know the names of their elders more often
than women do.

Table 3.45

Number of Informants Providing at Least One Name

	H	W
1 of 8 great-grandparents	0	3
2 of 8 great-grandparents	1	2
3 of 8 great-grandparents	2	6
4 of 8 great-grandparents	1	3
5 of 8 great-grandparents	0	1
6 of 8 great-grandparents	1	1
8 of 8 great-grandparents	0	2
1 of 16 great-great-grandparents . . .	0	1
2 of 16 great-great-grandparents . . .	1	0
4 of 16 great-great-grandparents . . .	1	0
7 of 16 great-great-grandparents . . .	0	1
14 of 16 great-great-grandparents . . .	0	1
Six generations back	0	1
Ten generations back	1	0

We tried to check for any tendencies of this sort, for if they existed they would be very important to know. But the Spearman r_s or rank correlation coefficient, the Kendall rank correlation coefficient (gau), and the Friedman two-way analysis of variance by ranks all show that the relationships between knowledge of names and genealogical category are basically the same for both male and female Egos. That is, while there may be great differences *within* any given genealogical category (as defined by generation and degrees of collateral removal) between the percentage whose first name is known by men and the percentage known by women, difference in the ranks of these percentages is not very great. We could put this in terms of the pattern of information loss, which we know increases with distance from Ego. The *pattern* of information loss in genealogical categories is the same for men and women, even though the actual *amount* of information loss is smaller for women in the most distant categories than it is for men.

VII. *Religious Affiliation*

Most of our informants reported that their kin universes were homogeneous in religious affiliation. More than 90% of those on any given genealogy were either Catholic, or Protestant, or Jewish. Additionally, if the kin universe of one spouse was homogeneous, usually the kin universe of the other spouse was homogeneous, and both had the same religion.

However, a small but distinct group of informants reported kin universes which were religiously heterogeneous. And, in one case, the religious affiliation of 90% was unknown. In the interviews, this group conveyed the impression that religious affiliation was unimportant. It does not follow, of course, that their characterization of religion was correct. But they presented a picture of a relatively coherent universe where religious affiliation was either absent or of minimal importance. These data are summarized in table 3.46.

So far, we have used both first name and religious affiliation as measures of our informant's knowledge about the members of their kin universes.

If we compare Ego's knowledge of Alter's first name with Ego's knowledge of Alter's religious affiliation, we can see that these are very different kinds of knowledge indeed (table 3.47).

First, let us recall that female informants knew the first names of more members of their kin universes than male informants. This male/female informant difference is not repeated here; instead, there is about the same percentage of "religious affiliation unknown" for male as for female Egos.

Second, the percentage of Alters whose religion is known is far higher, and consistently so, than that of Alters whose first name is known for each case. That is, Ego is far more likely to know the religious affiliation of a member of his kin universe than he is to know that person's first name.

We did not undertake certain statistical measures in dealing with knowledge of religious affiliation that we used in studying knowledge of first name. For instance, we showed that knowledge of first name drops off sharply beyond certain points of genealogical distance (pp. 59-66 above), just as knowledge of persons in those categories does. But since knowledge of religious affiliation is either very, very high (over 90% of the kin universe) or remarkably low (31%, 16%, 55%, etc.), it seems obvious that we are dealing with two very different kinds of things and that religious affiliation has certain meanings which knowledge of first name does not have. We have guessed that religious affiliation tends to be treated as a badge or mark of identity of the entire family, while knowledge of first name cannot have this function. Thus a family may see itself as predominantly Catholic, or Jewish, and there is a tendency to

Table 3.46

Religious Affiliation by Case and Sex of Informant
(Percentage of Totals Only)*

Case	Catholic		Protestant		Jewish		Unknown		Not Asked	
	M	F	M	F	M	F	M	F	M	F
03	2%	1%	0%	1%	98%	98%	0%	0%	0%	0%
04	0	0	5	0	95	100	0	0	0	0
06	96	98	2	0	0	0	1	1	1	1
09	100	97	0	0	0	0	0	3	0	0
10	0	0	0	1	99	99	1	0	0	0
11	1	0	1	1	93	96	3	2	2	1
13	0	*	100	*	0	*	0	*	0	*
14	1	2	48	29	0	0	51	69	0	0
15	71	48	0	8	0	0	29	39	0	5
16	0	0	81	90	0	0	19	10	0	0
17	0	0	0	0	100	95	0	3	0	2
19	0	7	100	93	0	0	0	0	0	0
22	25	*	33	*	0	*	41	*	0	*
23	84	*	11	*	1	*	2	*	2	*
24	0	0	8	15	0	0	90	84	2	2
26	0	0	0	3	100	96	0	0	0	1
28	99	*	1	*	0	*	0	*	0	*
29	1	*	0	*	61	*	38	*	0	*
30	0	1	100	96	0	0	0	0	0	3
31	84	95	16	0	0	0	0	1	0	4
33	28	9	35	62	0	0	31	26	1	4
36	98	100	0	0	2	0	0	0	0	0
37	44	0	30	68	0	0	26	31	0	0
39	0	5	100	95	0	0	0	0	0	0
42	0	0	0	0	98	96	2	2	0	2
43	5	8	65	37	0	1	26	45	4	9
44	0	0	1	0	96	100	3	0	0	0

* Only those cases where "Not Asked" equals 10% or less are included
here. Those marked with an asterisk in the table indicate that the
"Not Asked" category is more than 10%.

"extend" the coverage of this badge to all members where this is possible. Indeed, within the Jewish and the Catholic traditions, there
is a tendency to "drop" and not count members who marry "outside the
faith." But we have no clear way of measuring this, although we as-

Table 3.47

Knowledge of First Name and Knowledge
of Religious Affiliation
(N=49*)

Case	Ego Male		Ego Female	
	First Name Known	Religion Known	First Name Known	Religion Known
03	39%	100%	58%	100%
04	48	100	48	100
06	51	99	48	99
09	49	100	49	97
10	52	100	58	100
11	59	97	65	98
13	72	100	65	*
14	45	49	47	31
15	50	71	45	61
16	61	81	59	90
17	52	100	53	97
19	80	100	71	100
22	62	59	58	*
23	63	98	52	*
24	63	10	72	16
26	53	100	61	100
28	48	100	51	*
29	51	62	66	*
30	53	100	55	100
31	49	100	50	99
33	46	69	45	74
36	60	100	63	100
37	34	74	52	69
39	54	100	61	100
42	63	98	56	98
43	37	74	34	55
44	49	97	66	100

* Only cases where "Not Asked" equals 10% or less included in this
comparison. Those marked with an asterisk in the table indicate
that the "Not Asked" category is more than 10% and so no figures are
given.

sume that the tendency does operate. This same badge or marking function applies to the "religion unknown" category, of course, since these people are saying that religious affiliation is of no meaning or consequence to them and therefore they do not know what, if any, religious affiliations other members of their kin universe may have. This is certainly clear for certain of our informants, who stated it explicitly.

VIII. *Geographic Concentration*

Almost everyone who was reported by our informants as a living relative was also located--at least as being in one of the states or in a foreign country, even when the street number and town or city were not known. Knowledge of residence, then, did not prove to be a very useful measure of our informants' knowledge of their kin universes.

However, the degree of geographic concentration or dispersal of the members of a kin universe can be used in much the same way we used religious affiliation--as a measure of the homogeneity of the kin universe.

Information about geographic dispersal was obtained by asking each informant explicit questions, when the genealogy was collected, about where each Alter on the genealogy was living at the time, or, if the Alter were dead, where he was living when he died. The information thus does not tell us anything about how much moving Alter may have done over time--how often a given Alter may have moved or from where to where. Neither does it tell us if the notion of a "home town" or "roots in a place" may be important to a particular person in the kin universe or to the informant himself. The information about place of residence is simply Alter's location at the moment the genealogy was taken and should be interpreted to mean no more than that.

We use the forty-four genealogies provided by female informants and forty from their husbands.

The residence of each Alter is given on the genealogy as precisely as we could elicit it from the informant. It usually includes the names of the city or town and of the state. In coding this material, however, we distinguished only Chicago from its state. Otherwise, we coded only the state. We further grouped certain states together roughly by geographic distance from Chicago. In general, the code is as follows:

1. Chicago.
2. Illinois (not including Chicago), Wisconsin, Michigan, Indiana, Ohio, Kentucky, Missouri, Iowa, Minnesota.

3. North Dakota, South Dakota, Nebraska, Kansas, Oklahoma, Arkansas, Tennessee, West Virginia, Pennsylvania, New York.

4. Maine, Vermont, New Hampshire, Massachusetts, Rhode Island, Connecticut, New Jersey, Delaware, Maryland, District of Columbia, Virginia, Canada--eastern provinces.

5. North Carolina, South Carolina, Georgia, Alabama, Mississippi, Louisiana, Texas.

6. Montana, Wyoming, Colorado, New Mexico, Arizona, Utah, Idaho, Nevada.

7. Washington, Oregon, California, Florida, Hawaii, Alaska, Canada--western provinces, Mexico.

8. Middle and South America, Australia, Africa, British Isles, Europe.

The data presented in the following tables indicate that some of our informants' families are quite centralized. Four reported that at least 90% of their kin universe lived within one of our areas. However, some families were dispersed. Twenty informants reported that no more than 40% of their relatives lived within any single area. In general, most reported fairly centralized kin universes. Over half of our informants reported that more than half of their relatives lived within a single area.

We know that all of our informants lived in Chicago. In addition, seventeen men and fourteen women reported that more than 50% of their relatives lived in Chicago. It is interesting that the three women who reported the most centralized families (80% or more in one area) were married to men whose families were about as centralized.

Table 3.48

Percentage of Kin Universe in Most Populous Area

Percentage	Number of Men	Number of Women
90-100	2	2
80-89	5	1
70-79	4	10
60-69	5	7
50-59	8	9
40-49	6	5
30-39	10	9
20-29		1
0-19		

Furthermore, in twenty-three cases, the area which contained the highest percentage of husband's relatives was also the area with the highest percentage of the wife's family. The opposite was true in the other seventeen cases.

Table 3.49

Concentration of Kin Universe by Area

Number of Areas Required to =	Number of Cases							
	100%		90%		80%		70%	
	M	F	M	F	M	F	M	F
1			2	2	7	3	11	13
2	1		8	10	16	21	21	24
3	8	3	15	17	10	16	8	6
4	8	10	6	10	7	4		1
5	8	15	9	5				
6	8	9						
7	7	5						
8		2						
Total	40	44	40	44	40	44	40	44

IX. *Contact*

In collecting the genealogical material, we asked each informant a series of questions about his contact with each person listed on his genealogy. Here we shall consider the answers to those questions-- which relatives are contacted, by whom, and how.

This information will not tell us very much about the content of kinship relationships, for there is both more and less to relationships than indicated by contact. But it will add another dimension to our understanding of the internal structure of the kin universe.

We started with high hopes that, by doing a fine-grain study of contact, we would learn a good deal about the relationships between Ego and his relatives. Therefore we asked a series of finely honed questions and elicited as precise frequencies as we could. We divided contact into seeing and other forms (such as writing, telephoning, etc.). We then divided the seeing into voluntary occasions and formal ones, thereby distinguishing the spontaneous visit from the en-

counter at a wedding, a funeral, or another such event. We felt
this would differentiate important forms of contact. For example,
encountering a cousin at three different formal events (a wedding, a
funeral, and a confirmation) was not quite the same as going to visit
that cousin in his home on a voluntary, informal basis. By the same
token, we distinguished between sending and receiving formal announcements and invitations to formal events and sending and receiving
Christmas or New Year's or birthday cards. Thus we distinguished
voluntary face-to-face contact from those involuntary face-to-face
encounters at the same formal events. We further distinguished between contact by telephoning, writing letters, and sending holiday
and greeting cards and other notices and announcements. We then distinguished Ego's getting in touch with a specific Alter--Cousin John,
perhaps--from the situation in which Ego and his spouse would meet
Cousin John and his spouse, that is, family visits family, as dif-
ferentiated from person visits person. Finally, we drew fine distinctions between frequencies, eliciting information and coding frequencies from "no contact," "rare," "1-5," "6-10," "11-20," "21-30,"
"31-40," "41-50," and "51 and over" times a year.

Suffice it to say that our attempt at making such a fine-
grain analysis proved futile. This in itself is a finding of significance. In almost all cases, Ego had five or fewer contacts with
any Alter (except members of his own nuclear family) a year. And
rather than being able to make fine discriminations between different
kinds of voluntary and nonvoluntary contacts, we found that the frequencies were so small that we were forced to collapse the categories
into two, voluntary or nonvoluntary. The expected differences between writing, telephoning, and visiting did not emerge. And so, in
our analysis, we used the main categories of contact versus no contact, and voluntary versus nonvoluntary. Finally, where we tried to
discriminate between the situation where Ego communicated with particular Alter and the one where Ego and his spouse communicated with
an Alter and his spouse, the contact turned out to be an overwhelming-
ly couple-to-couple matter. Any detailed analysis of Ego's contact
with Alter was handicapped by this fact. It was thus impossible to
make any fine discriminations to show who might be communicating with
whom how often and under what circumstances.

We shall not reproduce our complex tables here, but our results are important as negative findings. On the whole, contact
seemed to be almost entirely husband and wife to husband and wife.
Overall, the frequency of contact was remarkably lower than we had
anticipated. As we have observed, the majority of our informants

Table 3.50

Case by Residence, as Percentage of Kin Universe
Area/Sex of Informant

Case	1 M	1 F	2 M	2 F	3 M	3 F	4 M	4 F	5 M	5 F	6 M	6 F	7 M	7 F	8 M	8 F
01	36%	37%	12%	26%	43%	14%	9%		1%	2%		2%	16%	19%		1%
02	71	42	49	33			3			4			16	20	3%	1
03	75	90	6							4			20	5	31	
04	23	6	9	7	6	7	11	74%						6		
05	*	53	*	23	*	7	4	3	*				*	12	*	1
06	72	72	54	11	6	8			5				5	8	4	1
07	61	5	41	39	6	12	8	30	2	2			31	6	6	5
08	59	13	31	58		7		6				8		8	10	
09	40	58	19	21	3	5	14	5	5	1		1	24	5		4
10	81	75	3	7	1	1	1	3		2		1	10	15		
11	28	36	55	7	1	4	7	19			2%		5	30	2	4
12	60	69	38	10											2	21
13	22	7	50	59		4		26					6	4	22	
14	48	36	38	36	1		2	14	5	1	2	1	4	12		
15	86	76	3	19						5			11			
16		3	45	3	7	17	14	67	16		14		5			9
17	39	66	9	6	33	4	2						18	24		
18		5	4	11	84	34	5	5			5	19	2	9		17
19	39	11	17	11	20	13	5			57	17		8	2		
20	54	47	8	6	8	3					30		8	41		

21	22	33	36	30	4	7	29	5	5		2	10	2	14	1
22	35	34	35	18	11	22	7	30	12	1
23	69	53	11	21	11	4	1	20	1
24		5	10	79	31	12	3	35	72	1
25	68	9	11	2	2	7	4	7	1
26		77	10	4	39	2	5	3	31	16
27	2		31	4	22	6	15	15	27	54
28	65	67	14	4	16	13
29	55	49	3	5	9	28	1	33	10
30	28	12	39	65	11	2	11	11
31	82	1	4	97	3	1
32	74	22	18	44	5	5	14	29
33	54		33	65	5	1	27
34	10	4	22	21	5	32	4	43	39
35	*	24	*	29	*	*	24	2	*	15
36	93	70	39	15	5	3	5	7
37	49	39		34	5		2		6	19
38	*	4	89	78	*	24	8		*	3
39		15	10		9	3	61	9	1	2	6
40				90		14	80	3
41	*	42	83	4	1	6	8	20	*	9	53	1
42	5	45	19	23	3	2	4	3	1	4	21	8	*
43	67	57		5	1	15	1	5	1	4	5	8	7
44	26	78	5	3	3	15	5	5	52	1	4
Total	39	24	9	7	3	2	10	13	2

* No genealogy collected.

had at most five contacts a year with Alter. And this, interestingly enough, held for families in which more than 50% of those in the genealogy resided in the Chicago area.

Finally, contact was scored only for living adult relatives domiciled separately. For example, a teen-ager living with his parents could not be counted, because any interaction he had with Ego could easily be a consequence of Ego's own contact preferences--not anything the teen-ager wanted.

With these considerations in mind, we can proceed with the data.

In general, informants of both sexes tended to get in touch with more female than male kinsmen, although this tendency seems stronger for female informants (see table 3.51). The exception to this generalization is formal events (weddings, funerals, etc.) where Ego has no control over who may attend.

Table 3.51

Probability That More Relatives on Mother's Side
Are Contacted Than on Father's Side, by Sex
of Informant and Mode of Contact

Mode of Contact	Ego Male	Ego Female
Visit	.500	.079
Telephone	.315 (F/M)[+]	.054*
Writing	.377	.017*
Contact[§]	.500	.003*
Formal occasion . . .	.090 (F/M)[+]	.500
Holiday cards	.271	.248

* The p value is statistically significant.
[+] The relationship is reversed; the probability is that more relatives on father's side are contacted.
[§] Any visit and/or telephone and/or written contact.

Women tend to get in touch with more relatives on the mother's side of the family than on the father's side. The same is probably not true of male informants. Nor does it obtain in formal occasions, although a formal event may involve primarily persons from one side or the other. The probabilities are given in table 3.52.

Table 3.52 suggests a strong female Ego to female Alter bias. Table 3.53 suggests a female Ego to Mother's side of the family bias. In table 3.53 we also combine these two elements and discover that the

Table 3.52

Probability That More Female Alters Than Male Alters
Are Contacted, by Sex of Informant
and Mode of Contact

Mode of Contact	Ego Male	Ego Female
Visit	.345	.0001*
Telephone	.227	.017*
Writing	.500	.005*
Contact[†]	.281	.0001*
Formal occasion . . .	.500	.072
Holiday cards	.419	.0002*

* The p value is statistically significant.
[†] Any visit and/or telephone and/or written contact.

most significant preference is that of female informants to contact
women on the mother's side.

Table 3.53

Probability That as Many Male Alters as Female Alters
Are Contacted, All Forms of Contact

	Father's Side	Mother's Side
Ego male	.192	.324
Ego female	.227	.002

Let us now turn from relatives who *are* contacted and consider
those who *could be*. Tables 3.54 and 3.55 show the proportions of
consanguineals contacted by generation and degree of collateral removal. Proportions are calculated by dividing the number of reported
living relatives by the number of relatives contacted. Thus, if
there are ten living individuals in a particular cell and eight of
them are contacted, that cell reads 80%.

Several conclusions can be drawn from these tables. First,
the overall pattern is reminiscent of the fade-out and drop-off
noted in our consideration of the proportion of relatives reported
in "Generation and Collateral Removal," above. Second, as with knowledge of first name, the relationship between the aunt/uncle and the

Table 3.54

Percentage Contacted of Those Available by Generation,
Collateral Removal, and Sex of Ego
(N=39)

	R^0 Ego M	R^0 Ego F	R^1 Ego M	R^1 Ego F	R^2 Ego M	R^2 Ego F	R^3 Ego M	R^3 Ego F
G^{+2}	50%	53%	15%	21%	20%	0%	*	*
G^{+1}	†	†	44	67	17	9	16%	22%
G^0	†	†	90	88	20	17	11	14
G^{-1}	†	†	34	42	4	7	*	0
G^{-2}	†	†	13	0	*	16	*	*

* No cases. 0% means that, of those available, none are contacted.
† Percentages not calculated, since they are not relevant here.

Table 3.55

Percentage Contacted of Those Available by Generation,
Removal, Sex of Ego, Sex of Alter
(N=39)

Alter		R^1 Male	R^1 Female	R^2 Male	R^2 Female	R^3 Male	R^3 Female
G^{+2}	Male	10%	7%				
	Female	19	29				
G^{+1}	Male	45	64	18%	2%		
	Female	42	69	15	15		
G^0	Male	91	90	12	16	5%	12%
	Female	89	86	21	23	17	17
G^{-1}	Male	39	23	3	5		
	Female	28	50	5	8		

nephew/niece categories is asymmetrical (see p. 63). That is, if
importance can be measured by the reported contact, the elders are
more important to the young than vice versa, for the young report
more contact with the older generation than the older generation report contact with the young. Third, in general, women report being
in touch with a higher percentage of relatives than men do. But
this pattern is not clear and may be more complex than we realize.
It is partially clarified by table 3.53, which again demonstrates
the clear female Ego to mother's side bias. However, we now know
that the bias becomes more marked at greater genealogical distance
from Ego.

We have noted that more women are contacted than men. Look-
ing at table 3.55, we note that this bias is also more marked for
more distant kinsmen for both male and female informants.

We have already presented our finding that female informants
contact their mother's side of the family preferentially. The combined effect of family side and sex was statistically significant
only for female Alter on mother's side (table 3.53). Tables 3.56
and 3.57 present the data by age of informant and then by generation
and degree of collateral removal. Table 3.58 is additionally divided, by the sex of the linking relative, for close kin.

Table 3.56

Proportion of Consanguineals Contacted
by Age of Informant

	Young	Middle	Old
Husbands . .	31.5%	24.6%	29.1%
Wives . . .	35.5	25.6	32.7

It might be expected that the geographic distance between
Ego and Alter would affect the proportion of relatives contacted.
However, as tables 3.60 and 3.61 indicate, this does not seem to be
the case for consanguineals. Only for four varieties of wives' relatives (G^{+1}, R^1 and ^{2}; G^0 R^1 and ^{2}) does increased distance lower
the proportion contacted.

The informant's age had the same effect on the proportion of
relatives contacted as it had on the number of relatives reported
(see table 3.56). Middle-aged informants contact slightly fewer of
their relatives than do either young or old informants.

Table 3.57

Percentage Contacted of Those Available by Generation,
Removal, Sex of Ego, and Side of Family
(N=39)

		R^1		R^2		R^3	
		M	F	M	F	M	F
G^{+2}	Fa side	18%	0%	*			
	Mo side	13	30				
G^{+1}	Fa side	46	56	15%	5%		
	Mo side	41	74	21	10		
G^0	Fa side	91†	90	25	16	0%	9%
	Mo side	89	86	14	24	39	18
G^{-1}	Fa side	27†	6		10		
	Mo side	39	68		4		

* Blank cells indicate that there are no instances where contact could occur or so few instances that percentages mean nothing.

† These two cells should *not* be read as "mother's side/father's side." Instead, the G^0R^1 cell contains brothers (father's side) and sisters (mother's side), while the $G^{-1}R^1$ cell contains brother's children (father's side) and sister's children (mother's side). These cells can be read as follows: male Egos contact 91% of all available brothers and 89% of all available sisters. Female Egos contact 90% of all available brothers and 86% of all available sisters. Male Egos contact 27% of all available brothers' children and 39% of all available sisters' children. Female Egos contact 6% of all available brothers' children, but 68% of all available sisters' children.

We could not consider age, family side, and generation and collateral removal simultaneously with contact because such subdivision yields such small numbers per cell as to be meaningless.

To summarize: our informants contacted more female relatives than male. Female informants contacted more relatives on their mother's side of the family than their father's--especially female Alters. This preference is more marked at greater genealogical distance from Ego. In general, however, the proportion of relatives contacted shows the same fuzzy boundary and drop-off with increasing genealogical distance that were noted in the numbers of relatives reported. Geographic distance does not seem to affect the proportion of relatives contacted. While middle-aged informants contacted the lowest percentage of their relatives, in all age-groups the wives contacted more of their relatives than the husbands did.

Table 3.58

Percentage Contacted of Those Available by Generation, Removal, Sex of Ego, Sex of Alter, and Side of Family

	Male		Female	
$G^{+1}R^1$, *Uncles, Aunts*				
Father's brother(s)	53%		65%	
Father's sister(s)	41		52	
Mother's brother(s)		39%		64%
Mother's sister(s)		44		83
G^0R^1, *Siblings*				
Brother(s)	91		90	
Sister(s)		86		83
G^0R^2, *Cousins*				
Father's sibling's son(s) . . .	22		15	
Father's sibling's daughter(s)	31		18	
Mother's sibling's son(s) . . .		14		17
Mother's sibling's daughter(s)		14		31
$G^{-1}R^1$, *Nepots*				
Brother's son(s)	40		0	
Brother's daughter(s)	17		13	
Sister's son(s)		39		60
Sister's daughter(s)		39		71
$G^{-1}R^2$, *Cousins' Children*				
Father's sibling's child's son	7		12	
Father's sibling's child's daughter	15		9	
Mother's sibling's child's son		0		0
Mother's sibling's child's daughter		0		8

X. Contact and Status Discrepancy

Each informant was asked to list the occupation of every person in his kin universe. O. D. Duncan's (1961) scale was used to transform occupations into status scores. Status differences were calculated by subtracting Alter's score from Ego's score on this scale. In this section, we shall present our findings on the importance of status discrepancy for contact between consanguineal kinsmen.

Table 3.59

Percentage Contacted of Those Available
by Kind of Cousin

	Ego Male	Female
Mother's sister's daughter . .	11%	30%
Mother's brother's daughter .	18	30
Mother's sister's son	18	17
Mother's brother's son	11	17
Father's sister's daughter . .	32	16
Father's brother's daughter .	24	19
Father's sister's son	23	5
Father's brother's son	22	24

As in the previous section, "contact" includes all the various forms of contact. We have grouped status score differences of less than twenty-nine as "mild discrepancy," and differences of thirty or more as "extreme discrepancy." We used the Wilcoxen test again to determine statistical significance.

Women were found to be more prone to contact kin whose status discrepancy was mild than with extremely discrepant kin (N=28, p=.0274). However, men did not show a significant preference (N=23, p=.2061).

Since women tend to contact more kin than men, it is not surprising that men do not contact significantly more extremely discrepant kin than women (N=22, p=.2514). Women are more prone to contact kin whose status discrepancy is mild (N=28, p=.0985).

As table 3.62 shows, men are more sensitive to status differences for male Alters than for female Alters, whereas women are equally sensitive to status discrepancy for both sexes.

In addition, we tested to determine whether status discrepancy affected the sending of holiday cards. No significant differences were found.

XI. Summary

We have presented in detail our findings about certain aspects of the American kin universe as these appear from our sample of informants. We shall now present a general picture and then review how the pattern varies for different kinds of informants.

Table 3.60

Proportion of All Consanguineals Contacted by Geographic
Location, Generation, and Collateral Removal

	R^0	R^1	Wives R^2	R^3	Area
G^{+2}	*	12.5%			1
	100.0%	20.0			2
		35.7			3-7
					8
G^{+1}	94.4	75.0	14.7%		1
	100.0		13.3		2
	100.0	66.7	6.4		3-7
		27.3			8
G^0		96.6	35.3	25.0%	1
		96.2	27.8	18.2	2
		80.8	18.3	23.5	3-7
			0.0		8
G^{-1}	100.0	25.0	10.0		1
		83.3	14.3		2
		42.9	12.0		3-7
					8

Key: Area 1 = Chicago
      Area 2 = Midwest
      Area 3-7 = North America
      Area 8 = Elsewhere
      See pp. 70-71.

* Blank cells indicate less than 5 relatives.

As we have said, there are two sides to American kin relationships. A kinsman is someone who is related (a) by blood or by
marriage, and (b) with whom Ego shares an interpersonal relationship.
Because our informants reported only a finite subset of their potential kin universes, each selected Alter must have certain qualifica-
tions in one or both of these areas. We shall attempt to draw a
general picture of those who have been chosen, according to our mea-
surements of their formal (or, loosely, genealogical) and their interpersonal qualities.

First, we shall review the formal characteristics of the

Table 3.61

Proportion of All Consanguineals Contacted by Geographic
Location, Generation, and Collateral Removal

	R^0	R^1	R^2	R^3	Area
			Husbands		
G^{+2}	100.0%	6.2%			1
	*				2
		60.0			3-7
					8
G^{+1}	100.0	37.0	20.0%		1
	100.0	58.3			2
	100.0	42.9	30.0	20.0%	3-7
			0.0		8
G^0		90.9	24.5	0.0	1
		66.7	18.3	50.0	2
		100.0	27.1	14.3	3-7
			0.0		8
G^{-1}		36.0	5.6		1
		36.4	14.3		2
		18.2	0.0		3-7
					8

Key: Area 1 = Chicago
      Area 2 = Midwest
      Area 3-7 = North America
      Area 8 = Elsewhere
      See pp. 70-71.

* Blank cells indicate less than 5 relatives.

members of our informants' kin universes. Only two simple measures
are available, type (consanguinity and affinity) and distance (generation and collateral removal). In addition, we can take size as a
compound measure, for a kin universe can be enlarged beyond a certain minimum only by including more distantly related relatives. We
shall also consider differences between sides of the family as indicating formal or genealogical distinction.

      Second, we shall review what we have discovered about the
interpersonal aspect of kinship relationships. These are knowledge
of Alter's first name, of whether Alter is alive or dead, of Alter's

85

Table 3.62

Contact by Status Discrepancy
and Sex of Alter and of Ego

| | Alter | |
	Male Mild SD	Female Mild SD
Ego male	N=20 p=.0934	N=16 p=.3669
Ego female	N=15 p=.0708	N=18 p=.0793

religion, Ego's contact with Alter, status discrepancy between Alter and Ego, and sex of link and of Alter. Our treatment of sex and side of the family is, perhaps, arbitrary. However, we feel that the importance of the sex of Alter and of link derives from the different types of interpersonal relationships between and within the sexes. On the other hand, side of the family reflects the more formal position of Alter.

The major distinctions among our informants are those of age and sex. Differences between men and women and between the old, middle-aged, and young informants will be highlighted.

Further, the variety and variability within our sample will be, of necessity, underemphasized. This is a brief and general summary of the results of a preliminary study. It should be remembered that the differences within each category were large compared with differences between categories, indicating that there are many unrecognized factors. We shall therefore repeat the ranges along with the averages here.

Our informants reported an average of 159 relatives apiece. The largest kin universe contained 468 members, and the smallest 23. The average comprised 72 consanguineals, 31 spouses of consanguineals (CA), and 56 of their consanguineals and their spouses (CAC+). The range for these categories was large--13-218, 4-106, and 0-279, respectively.

Consanguineals less than three degrees of generational and/or collateral removal distant from Ego were fairly completely reported (about 90%-100%). Very few consanguineals more than three steps distant were reported (0%-1%) of those possible. There was a fuzzy boundary of categories for which there was partial reporting (6%-49%

of potential). The same pattern seems to govern CAs and CAC+s, most of whom are linked through consanguineals close to Ego.

Overall, very slightly more consanguineals were reported on mother's side of the family than on father's.

Women reported larger, more extensive, and more asymmetrical kin universes than men did. The average size for women was 183, as opposed to 135 for men; the ranges were 35-468 and 23-314, respectively. Four of the five smallest universes were reported by men; four of the six largest were reported by women. While both men and women reported almost the same number of close relatives, women reported two to three times as many relatives who were three or more steps distant. Furthermore, a woman showed a bias in favor of her mother's side of the family, reporting about one-quarter again as many relatives as on her father's side. This bias was quite marked for distant relatives. The reverse bias was found among men. A woman reported an average of 8.9 distant kin on her father's side and 15.6 on her mother's, while for male informants the averages were 8.2 and 4.1, respectively. Overall, men reported about equal numbers of relatives on each side.

Older informants reported more relatives than younger ones. Among women, the average size increased from 117 for young informants through 175 for the middle-aged to 259 for the old informants. Men exhibited an increase from 85 through 147 to 179. Our three largest kin universes were reported by old women, and two of the five smallest by young men. For men, increasing age tended to increase the proportion of CAC+ and decrease the proportion of consanguineals. For women, increasing age seemed to increase the proportion of CA and CAC+. Overall, however, men and women reported the same proportions of C, CA, and CAC+. For all informants, young informants reported more consanguineals who belonged to the generations above their own, while old informants reported more consanguineals in the generations below their own.

In general, our informants seemed to maintain closer interpersonal relationships with their nearer and more directly related kin. More first names were known, the dead were reported and the dates of their death were known more often, and more of them were contacted. Geographic distance did not affect this tendency. In addition, informants appeared to maintain closer ties with relatives of their own sex.

Approximately 22% of the consanguineals and spouses of consanguineals reported were dead, while only 17% of the CAC+ were dead. The date of death was known exactly for 7% of the consanguineals but for only 5.5% of CA and 2.5% of CAC+.

First names for 66% of the consanguineals were known, but only for 56% of CA and 32% of CAC+. The first names of more than 80% of close consanguineals were known, but usually for less than 40% of the distant consanguineals. At all distances, names of consanguineals were known more often than names of their spouses.

Both men and women reported more consanguineals of the same sex as the link than of the opposite sex. Linked through father and brother were 1,321 men (614 by husbands, 707 by wives) and only 1,079 women (524 by husbands and 555 by wives). Linked through sisters and mothers, however, were 1,434 women (598 by husbands, 836 by wives) and only 1,250 men (520 by husbands, 730 by wives). Overall, only slightly more male (2,571) than female (2,513) consanguineals were reported.

The same general pattern is discerned when we consider the proportion of relatives who are contacted. More close consanguineals are contacted than distant ones. The proportion declines from 90% for quite close kinsmen to 0% for the most distant. Overall, more women are contacted than men.

Female (but not male) informants are significantly more prone to contact female kin whose status is only mildly discrepant from Ego's own than female kin whose status is extremely discrepant. Both sexes contact significantly more mildly discrepant male kin.

In addition, female informants contact a greater proportion of the consanguineals on their mother's side of the family than on their father's. Women also contact significantly (p=.002) more women than men on the mother's side. This was not true on the father's side; nor did men seem to exhibit any preferences, either by sex of Alter or by side of the family.

The sex of the informant does not markedly affect the proportion of dead persons in the kin universe, the proportion whose dates of death are known, or the proportion whose first names are known.

However, interest in (or at least knowledge of) the kin universe does appear to reach a low point in Ego's middle years. Middle-aged informants report fewer dead persons and fewer first names and contact fewer consanguineals than either other age-group.

Most of our informants (thirty-two of forty) reported kin universes which were homogeneous in religious affiliation, and both the husband and the wife assigned at least 90% of their relatives to one faith. The other cases seem to represent families to whom religion was not very important. In all but two cases, the religious affiliation of Alter was known more often than Alter's first name.

Many informants reported that most of their relatives lived in one geographic area. Twenty-four of 40 men and 29 of 44 women reported more than 50% in one area, while two men and two women reported 90% or more in one area. All but one informant had at least 30% of their relatives living in one of eight regions. Overall, men and women reported about equally concentrated kin universes.

Thus far, we have devoted much space to reviewing the differences between male and female informants in terms of *magnitudes* and *quantities*. While we have discussed pattern in very general terms, we have slighted the conclusion obvious from table 3.63--the *pattern* of our data is very similar for men and women.

Under each of the seven variables at the top of the table are are the ranks of the most important G/R cells, listed at left. The cell which contained the highest value was assigned the rank of 1, and the highest rank number in the column was assigned to the cell with the lowest meaningful value. Thus, despite the great differences in the magnitude of the values in the cells (described at length above) between men and women, the quite clear coincidences in rank between the sexes for each of the variables demonstrates that the same system and pattern govern both men and women.

NOTES

1. We have eliminated step-, half-, foster, and link unknown kin, as noted in chapter 2.

2. This indicator was first suggested by Raymond Firth when he compared what he once called "known" and "nominated" kin (Firth 1956: 45). Since then, he has preferred to call these "named" and "unnamed" (Firth et al. 1970:155).

Table 3.63

Ranks of Male and Female Informants on Each of Seven Variables
by Generation and Collateral Removal Cell
Variables A to G*

GR Cell	A Ego		B Ego		C Ego		D Ego		E Ego		F Ego		G Ego	
	M	F	M	F	M	F	M	F	M	F	M	F	M	F
$G^{+2}R^0$					5	8					2	3	11	11
$G^{+2}R^1$	6	6	7	6	8	7	5	4			9	6	10	10
$G^{+1}R^0$					12	12							8	8
$G^{+1}R^1$	4.5	3	2	3	3	3	2	2	2	2	3	2	9	9
$G^{+1}R^2$	4.5	5	5	5	6	4	3	3			7	10	7	7
$G^{+1}R^3$											8	5		
G^0R^1	1	1	1	1	9	10	4	5	1	1	1	1	6	5
G^0R^2	3	4	4	4	2	2	1	1	3	3	5.5	7	5	6
G^0R^3	8	8			7	5	8	7					4	4
$G^{-1}R^1$	2	2	3	2	4	6	7	8	4	4	4	4	2.5	2
$G^{-1}R^2$	7	7	6	7	1	1	6	6					1	2
$G^{-1}R^3$	9	9			13	11							2.5	2
$G^{-2}R^1$					11	13								
$G^{-2}R^2$					10	9								

* Variables:
A = % Named consanguineals (C)
B = % Named consanguineals' affinals (CA)
C = Number of consanguineals (C) reported
D = Number of consanguineals' affinals (CA) reported
E = Number of consanguineals' affinals' consanguineals (CAC+) reported
F = Percentage contacted
G = Percentage reported alive

Chapter 4: CONCLUSIONS

This pilot study of the urban white middle-class American kin universe, using informants in Chicago, was undertaken as part of a larger investigation of the cultural aspects of American kinship. Although we have processed, analyzed, and reported these data separately, our methods and aims here have been very much influenced by the objectives of the larger investigation.

What does this study of the American kin universe by genealogical methods contribute to our understanding of the cultural aspects of American kinship? And how do these findings relate to those already reported? (Schneider 1968.)

It will be recalled that we have drawn a distinction between the kin universe and the category of "relatives" or "family." The latter category was a subset of the kin universe chosen by Ego.

We did not systematically compare the kin universe with the universe of relatives for each of our informants. In retrospect, this appears to have been a flaw in our work. However, it is our impression that, for all practical purposes, the universe of relatives for any given Ego is very much like the kin universe--except that a few members of the kin universe are excluded, mainly distant kin. Other exclusions seem to be random. The distinction nevertheless remains important, in that the rules governing who can properly be included in the category of "relative" are not identical with the rules we used in defining the kin universe. However, the net effect seems to be so small that, for present purposes, we can use the two terms interchangeably.

We learned the rules for inclusion in the category of relatives partly through the general interviews and partly through the genealogical inquiry by bringing to the informant's attention questions that arose from the genealogy as they applied to his more general statements. Thus we were able to ask his definition of a relative and discuss this in general terms. Then we could go to the genealogy and ask about particular persons and why they were or were not considered to be relatives.

The general rule was given abstractly in the interviews--

91

anyone related by blood or by marriage was a relative. But inquiry
clarified what was meant by "blood" and "marriage" and brought out
the fact that blood was itself considered to be both a sharing of
natural biogenetic substance and a code for conduct enjoining diffuse
enduring solidarity, while marriage was variously defined. It could
be the marriage of Ego alone or the marriage of any of Ego's consanguineals. It could also include the relationship of anyone through
the marriage of either Ego or any of his consanguineals (for example,
spouse's mother, or the marriage that related Ego to his mother's
brother's wife's sister and perhaps even her husband). "Marriage"
was also used to mean a kind of relationship interpreted as one enjoining diffuse enduring solidarity. It was then used as the expres-
sion par excellence of that kind of relationship, so that marriage
in its special sense of a legal union need not obtain--only a relationship of that kind.

The genealogical study itself confirms the rules for inclusion in the category of relative. "Relatives" may be related through
ties of blood or by marriage as the spouse of Ego. But certain persons considered to be relatives by our informants are not related by
blood to Ego or by marriage as his spouse or through his spouse.
They are, rather, related through their marriage to one of Ego's
consanguineals (CA). Others are related as the consanguineals of
those (CAC and CAC+), as are still others to whom no relationship
can be traced through such routes. By no means all of those to whom
relations of blood are traced are considered to be relatives. The
fact that a relationship of blood can be traced does not in and of
itself necessarily mean that the person involved will be included in
the category of relative.

The category of relatives is culturally divided into those
who are "close" and those who are "distant." This internal differentiation in terms of "distance" is clearly reflected in the structure of the kin universe. Indeed, it is one of the fundamental fea-
tures of that structure. We shall approach the category of distant
relatives through discussing the boundary of the category of relative. We shall continue with a discussion of "close" relatives and
then proceed to a discussion of "distance" in general as this illu-
minates our findings.

From the fact that, when an informant is asked directly who
his relatives are, he responds that a relative is anyone related by
blood or by marriage, it would seem that there is a clear-cut closure
rule. A person either is or is not related by blood or marriage.
If he is, he is a relative; if he is not, he is not a relative. How-

ever, this direct reply does not yield the full rule. In fact, the
genealogical inquiry shows that there is no clear, precise rule for
closure that can be stated in genealogical or in any other terms.
For example, in a unilineal descent category that is agnatic, whether
a person is included or excluded depends entirely on his ability to
trace an agnatic link through an ascendant to other members of that
category. But other systems (not necessarily unilineal) may still
have precise closure rules. For example, the category may include
all those who are second cousins or closer but no one who is beyond
that genealogical range. Other systems may use closure rules such
as coresidence or coownership of property. But the American category of relatives has no single, specific closure rule.

Closure rules define the boundary of the unit. Where a precise closure rule obtains, the unit's boundary is clear and unambig-
uous. But since the American category of relatives has no such closure rule, the boundary can be variable not only from informant to
informant but also for any given informant at different times. The
informant alone has the option of including or excluding persons.
This does not mean that every person can behave in a purely arbitrary
or capricious way, nor does it mean that his actions are random.
There are certain conditions that figure with greater or lesser
weight in his decisions about inclusion and exclusion. We shall
touch on these below.

First, however, let us state our findings about the boundary
of the kin universe--which is simply another way of talking about
the cultural category of "distant" relatives.

The boundary of the kin universe can be described from one
point of view as "fuzzy" precisely because of the lack of any clear,
single rule of closure. As we have indicated, it was to be expected--
and we indeed found--that the kin universes of different informants
would not be identical in range and kinds of genealogically distant
categories they included. Nor were numbers or proportions in these
categories the same for different informants. We did not compare
the kin universes of the same person at different periods and so
cannot address that question directly. However, the impression we
received from the interviews suggests that, at the outer edges, at
the boundary, persons could be added or dropped as the occasion required, and that our informants did so.

But when the boundary is examined closely, the fuzziness re-
solves into an area that first recedes and then drops off sharply
as genealogical distance increases. This area in the kin universes
of our white middle-class urban Chicago Americans occurred from the

third and fourth squares from Ego on the generation-collateral removal chart we used. The evidence of fading and drop-off can be
discerned most clearly by comparing the values for the number of
relatives who could be expected to be in these squares with the number actually reported. For these boundary squares, only a very small
proportion of those expected are actually reported. For example, we
estimate that, of the number of second cousins who are likely to exist for our population of informants, at most about 6% are actually
reported.

If the boundary area represents "distant" relatives, then the
the core area represents "close" relatives. We found that all or
very nearly all of those close relatives who could be expected to
exist were reported. (We speak only of consanguineals, for the moment.) The measure of this statement remains the material from table
3.20.

In other words, the inclusion rule--a relative is a person
related by blood or by marriage--seems to work perfectly for close
blood relatives, and no other considerations need be invoked to deal
with exceptions or variations. But where distant relatives are concerned, the inclusion rule does not account for those excluded.
There is no exclusion rule that explains why those who would seem to
be covered by the inclusion rule are excluded. Further, the rule
that anyone related by blood or marriage is a relative as simply
stated in abstract terms by informants is insufficient to account
for those who are actually included.

To understand this, we must recall that the categories of
"close" and "distant" are parts of a general cultural conception of
distance. What, then, does "distance" mean and how is it expressed
in the structure of the kin universe? Let us turn now to this problem.

We must begin with the fundamental definition of a relative
as anyone related by blood or by marriage. Here, "blood" means two
things: relationship of biogenetic substance, and code for conduct
enjoining diffuse enduring solidarity. Marriage is a relationship
of diffuse enduring solidarity, but it lacks the aspect of biogenetic
substance.

Since blood is a substance, it is divisible. A person shares
100% of his blood with full siblings and derives half from each parent. Cousins share proportionally less, since (unless they are dou-
ble cousins, of course) they share the substance of only one parent
and not the other. And so, with each genealogical step away from
Ego, less and less substance is shared. Since there is no closure

rule, there is no particular point at which the sharing of substance necessarily changes to a state of nonsharing or becomes trivial. Thus some of our informants traced a relationship between themselves and a famous person whom they had never met and with whom they had never associated--and who was probably unaware of their existence-- simply on the ground that there was a blood tie, however remote.

Distance, then, is in one of its aspects simply the calibration of the proportion of blood shared by two relatives.

Blood, however, also means a relationship of diffuse enduring solidarity. But blood as substance and blood as code for conduct are hierarchically ranked, so that blood takes precedence in many situations. Thus a blood relationship is usually marked by an interpersonal relationship of some sociability. Even if it is not, it will, in most situations, still "count" for more than the interpersonal relationship. Thus it is possible to be disowned by a parent, to "disown" a parent, never to see or have any social intercourse at all with a parent, yet to list that parent on one's genealogy.

This hierarchical relationship between blood as substance and as code for conduct accords with the fact that "close" consanguineal relatives tend to be fully or almost fully reported, while "distant" consanguineal relatives tend to be underreported--if they are reported at all. Indeed, more often than not, they are not reported, since they are not even known to exist. (See chapter 3, section on "Generation and Collateral Removal," above.)

The hierarchical relationship between blood as substance and blood as code for conduct is reiterated in the relationship between blood and marriage, for marriage is simply the code for conduct without the substantive (biogenetic) element. But once again, although this hierarchical relationship obtains in many normatively defined situations, it may be reversed in certain specific situations. For example, the bond between husbands and wives in our middle-class sample was regarded by our informants as taking precedence over the bond between parent and child, even though the latter is a bond of substance and the former is not.

The relationship between blood as substance plus code and marriage as code without substance is interesting in another respect that bears directly on our findings about the structure of the kin universe.

In one sense there either is or is not a substantive relationship. Yet we have seen that distance is the precise calibration of how much substance is presumed to be shared between Ego and any relative. This degree of substance is important for distinguishing closer from more distant consanguineal relatives. In another sense, however, these values are reversed, for there either is or is not a "relationship" of diffuse enduring solidarity. Further, there is the question of Ego's option to act as against a "given" attribute over which Ego has no option. Where blood as substance either is or is not, it is something over which Ego can exercise no options. On the other hand, relationship as code for conduct is precisely something over which Ego is free to exercise his option, for, even when he is constrained by the fact that there "is" a blood relationship, he need not opt for the code for conduct.

The net effect, therefore, is that, as genealogical distance increases from Ego, more and more weight is thrown on the hierarchically subordinate aspects and on those that permit Ego to exercise more freely such options as he wishes. This is perhaps the fullest statement of "distance" in American kinship. It should not be equated simply with degrees of blood or of generation and collateral removal alone, for it entails the hierarchical ranking of blood and marriage, between blood as substance and blood as code for conduct, as well as the locus of Ego's option to act compared to Ego's lack of any freedom of choice.

Let us put this matter in yet another way. All relatives are distinguished from nonrelatives. Therefore all relatives have something in common, something which makes them "the same." It is this which probably accords with the homogeneity we found in the kin universes, especially in religion and probably in geographic locale. These seem to be two important ways of marking the "kindness," the "oneness" of the kin universe.

But if we consider only the category of relatives, we can immediately see that the differences between relatives can be summed up by distinguishing the closer from the more distant. The closer the relative, the more important it is that he is related by blood or marriage. The greater the genealogical distance, the more important nongenealogical and nonkinship considerations become, the more choice Ego has over whether to include or exclude Alter from his kin universe and whether to transmit Alter to his children.

The kin universe, then, has a hard core of close relatives. But it is elastic to some degree, even at this core, for different Egos and different kinds of Alters as well as for any given Ego or Alter over time. This elasticity is another statement of the great differences between informants, the differences in size and in the proportions of C, CA, and CAC+, and other differences between our male and female and our older and younger informants. It is, therefore, likely to be elastic for all the social variables, such as age, sex, class, occupation, ethnicity, religion, income, etc., that tend to influence the inclusion or exclusion decisions of different kinds of Egos about different kinds of Alters--particularly distant ones. The kin universe is elastic even at the core, but it is most elastic for distant relatives.

But although the kin universe is elastic, its structure remains constant regardless of the age, sex, and--we suggest--the occupation, class, ethnicity, religion, etc., of Ego. It may be larger or it may be smaller. It may go back more generations and further in time, or it may be shallower. It may extend to more collateral lines or be restricted to fewer. It may extend its scope to include more distant kin as distant consanguineals, persons married to these, or the consanguineals of these (C, CA, CAC+), or it may keep its scope to a minimum. When it does, the CAC+ will be most sharply curtailed, then the CA, and then the C. But the kin universe always has a firm core of close relatives. This core may expand to three squares from Ego or contract to just one square from Ego on the generation-collateral removal chart. That is, elasticity will be most evident at the juncture between close and distant relatives and in the distant relatives. But whatever the elasticity, the boundary structure will be the same; it will recede and then drop off sharply. This structure seems given by the rules governing what a relative is and the rules for inclusion, exclusion, and closure, as they are culturally stated.

Correspondingly, the measures of "relationship," such as contact, accord with this structure. Ego knows more first names of close kin than of distant kin. He knows more dates of death for close kin than for distant kin. Contact--visiting, etc.--is proportionally "closer" with closer relatives. Even such an apparent anomaly as the fact that religion is more often known for distant kin than is first name is understandable in light of these considerations: if religion is the mark of a "kind of family" and a "family" is a "kind," this fact makes sense.

We have spoken of "close" and "distant" relatives but have been careful not to provide any definition of these categories in terms of generation-collateral removal cells or in such terms as "uncle-aunt" or "first cousin." Our reason is simply that the definition varies not only for various populations but also from informant to informant within our sample. Yet the variation is not random but, rather, elastic, as we have been suggesting. Certainly parents, siblings, and children are "close." The categories of uncle-aunt and nephew-niece present special problems. The category of children presents a special methodological problem for this study. We shall return to the last two points shortly.

Operationally, all or nearly all "close" relatives who are likely to exist are reported. Usually, even those who are dead are reported. There is generally no mother's side or father's side bias in reporting them. Their first names are known. And so on and so forth. But this is merely to repeat what we have already found. When aunts-uncles, first cousins, nephews-nieces, grandparents, grand- children are largely all reported, etc., then they are obviously "close." When they are rarely reported, their first names rarely known, etc., then they are distant. Again, there is no rigid cate- gorical rule that says, for example, "all those genealogically closer than first cousins count as close relatives."

Indeed, this is just the problem we see in our sample in the uncle-aunt and nephew-niece categories. For some informants, the uncle-aunt category is close; for others, it is distant. Thus we cannot say that clearly for our sample the uncle-aunt category is or is not close. Furthermore, there is a marked asymmetry in the uncle- aunt and nephew-niece categories. This was remarked in Schneider 1968 and is borne out in the empirical work reported here. The loss in the uncle-aunt category is moderately high; the loss in the nephew- niece category is much greater. Of course, by the time Ego is inter- viewed, he has all the uncles and aunts he is ever likely to have, but the same cannot be said about his nephews and nieces. On the whole, however, our impression is that the uncle-aunt category is closer than the nephew-niece category, despite the fact that every Ego who reports an uncle or an aunt must be a nephew or a niece.

Finally, let us make another point explicit. The kin uni- verse is an Ego-oriented unit with interlocking and overlapping mem- berships with every other Ego's kin universe, for every Ego will be close kin to some and distant kin to others and not kin to others. Thus a kin universe can be defined only for a given person. No two kin universes are the same in fact. Nor can they be even in prin- ciple, given the options open to Ego for choices and selections about inclusion and exclusion. Indeed, the genealogies we took from full siblings show that even the kin universes of full siblings show marked differences in content, since each has dropped some kin which the other has included or included some which the other has dropped or not remembered or never known.

We can now see just how the elasticity of the kin universe operates within the structure we have outlined, by considering, first,

the informant's age, and second, the informant's sex and that of link
and Alter, as variables. We think we have held class constant for
our white middle-class Chicago sample.

Age of informant seems to be important primarily to the overall size of the kin universe. Since size is increased primarily by
increasing the CA and CAC+, these categories are larger for our older
informants (assuming that the birth rate is held constant, of course,
for the sheer size of the kin universe is in part a function of the
birth rate). Older women particularly report a larger proportion of
consanguineals in the generations below their own. Interestingly,
informants in their middle years (neither old nor young, by our stan-
dards) report fewer dead, fewer first names, and contact with fewer
consanguineals than the other age-groups.

Age, then, does not seem to be a very important variable for
our informants (except as noted above). The image of the old folks
sitting about and doing nothing but counting kin and dwelling on
their relatives does not get much support from our study.

Sex, on the other hand, does seem important, although this
may in part be a function of our having studied it in more detail.

To begin with, we encountered a host of folksy hypotheses
among our informants, our colleagues, our fieldworkers, and others
about male-female differences. We did not encounter such hypotheses
about age. One form these hypotheses took was that of "mother's side"
versus "father's side." Another was the firm assertion that women
were more "interested in" kinship than men and that women really knew
more and did more about kinship than men. Another was the statement
that there was a "matrilateral bias." A variant was supplied by the
informants who said, "Oh, don't talk to me about that sort of thing;
see my wife, she knows all about it"--in other words, the wife knows
more about "the family" than her husband and even, on occasion, the
wife knows more about her husband's family than her husband knows.

Alas! None of these hypotheses got much support in the form
in which we received them and have repeated them here. Yet sex seems
to be a very important variable, but in a very complex set of ways.

As our discussion of close versus distant relatives showed,
both men and women reported almost the same number of close relatives.
But women reported two to three times more distant relatives (three
or more steps away). Were these on the mother's side? Men and women
reported slightly more relatives through the mother than through the
father, but the difference was not great. But women reported about
one-quarter again as many relatives through the mother as through
the father. The bias was most marked for distant relatives rather

than close relatives. The reverse bias for distant relatives was shown by men, who reported more distant kin through the father than through the mother. But if we combine distant and close relatives, men did not show any bias toward either mother's or father's side.

If we now consider Alter, the picture becomes sharper in some ways. The strongest tendency is for women to report more female Alters through female links (through mothers and sisters). While men tended to report more men through male links, this tendency is not so strongly marked as the female-female-female one.

Female informants contact a greater proportion of their consanguineals on the mother's side than on the father's, and with significantly more female than male Alters on the mother's side. Men, however, do not show these contact biases, either through father or to male Alters.

What is not affected by the sex of the informant? The proportion of dead in the kin universe, the proportion whose dates of death are known, and the proportion whose first names, religion, and/ or geographic location are known.

Thus, even though women reported more kin than their husbands did (and it must not be forgotten that our female informants had twice the opportunity to report that their husbands did, since we had twice as many interviews with wives as with their husbands), this is not only a simple function of their being women. It is also a function of the sex of Alter and the sex of the link of Alter and the mother's side of the family for the women informants. Neither is the situation simply reversed for men--there is no such strong bias for men through the father to male Alters.

It is not possible to say, then, that there is a general "mother's side-father's side" distinction. There is a matrilateral bias for women; there is a slight patrilateral bias for men. Nor can we say that women just know more, take more interest in, and keep more in touch with, kin than men do. Although we have reported the general tendencies here, as we have tried to stress throughout, the individual differences are great. In our population, for example, some men knew more, got in touch with more, and reported more in general--and more distant kin in particular.

We do not feel that this is the place to venture any hypotheses to explain the sex differences among our informants' kin universes, since our primary aim was to get some idea about what the kin universes of our white middle-class Chicago informants are like. And this we have reported in detail.

REFERENCES

Duncan, O. D.
    1961 A Socio-Economic Index for All Occupations, and Properties
          and Characteristics of the Socio-Economic Index. In *Occupa-
          tion and Social Status*, A. J. Reiss, Jr., ed. New York:
          The Free Press.

Firth, R.
    1956 *Two Studies of Kinship in London*. London: London School of
          Economics, Monographs on Social Anthropology, No. 15.

Firth, R., Hubert, J., and Forge, A.
    1970 *Families and Their Relatives*. London: Routledge & Kegan
          Paul.

Hubert, J., Forge, A., and Firth, R.
    1967 Methods of Study of Middle-Class Kinship in London. Occa-
          sional paper, Department of Anthropology, London School of
          Economics.

Schneider, D. M.
    1965 American Kin Terms and Terms for Kinsmen: A Critique of
          Goodenough's Componential Analysis of Yankee Kinship Termi-
          nology. *American Anthropologist* 67(no. 5, pt. 2):288-308.

    1968 *American Kinship: A Cultural Account*. Englewood Cliffs,
          N. J.: Prentice-Hall.

Wolf, L.
    1964 Anthropological Interviewing in Chicago. Department of
          Anthropology, University of Chicago. Available through
          Photoduplication Department, Regenstein Library Microfilm
          #N3632.